SCIENCE SURPRISES!

Ready-to-Use Experiments & Activities for Young Learners

Jean R. Feldman, Ph.D.

MW01048270

Illustrations by

Rebecca Feldman Foster

THE CENTER FOR APPLIED RESEARCH IN EDUCATION
West Nyack, New York 10994

Library of Congress Cataloging-in-Publication Data

Feldman, Jean R., 1947–
    Science surprises! : ready-to-use experiments & activities for
young learners / Jean R. Feldman.
       p. cm.
    Includes index.
    ISBN 0-87628-871-9
    1. Science—Experiments.   2. Science—Study and teaching
(Elementary)—Activity programs.   I. Title.
    Q164.F35   1995   95-32272
    507.8—dc20   CIP

Printed in the United States of America

10 9 8 7 6 5 4 3

ISBN 0-87628-871-9

**THE CENTER FOR APPLIED RESEARCH
IN EDUCATION**
West Nyack, NY 10994
A Simon & Schuster Company

On the World Wide Web at http://www.phdirect.com

Prentice-Hall International (UK) Limited, *London*
Prentice-Hall of Australia Pty. Limited, *Sydney*
Prentice-Hall Canada Inc., *Toronto*
Prentice-Hall Hispanoamericana, S.A., *Mexico*
Prentice-Hall of India Private Limited, *New Delhi*
Prentice-Hall of Japan, Inc., *Tokyo*
Simon & Schuster Asia Pte. Ltd., *Singapore*
Editora Prentice-Hall do Brasil, Ltda., *Rio de Janeiro*

This book is dedicated to John,
my husband, my friend.

ACKNOWLEDGMENTS

A special thanks to all of my friends who suggested ideas and experiments for SCIENCE SURPRISES! Patti Guy, a former student, shared so many special ways to help children learn about nature. Cheri Hillier contributed the activities for discovery boxes, as well as many other ideas. Dr. Tom Feldman, my brother-in-law, reviewed the "explanations," and my dear sister-in-law, Rebecca Feldman, illustrated the book so delightfully. And I never would have been able to accomplish this task without the encouragement of my editor, Susan Kolwicz.

I also wish to thank all the children I have known who have stared in awe at a rainbow, gathered wildflowers for me, giggled when they caught a cricket, wondered at a growing seed, and believed that science and the world in which we live truly are magic.

ABOUT THE AUTHOR

Jean Feldman has been a teacher in the Atlanta area for over 25 years. Currently she is an instructor in the Early Childhood Department at DeKalb Technical Institute. Dr. Feldman has a B.A. from the University of Georgia, a D.A.S.T. from Emory University, and a M.A. and Ph.D. from Georgia State University. She is a member of the National Association for the Education of Young Children, Georgia Association for Young Children, and the Georgia Preschool Association. Dr. Feldman presents to professional groups across the country, and serves on the board of several organizations. She is the author of two books published by the Center for Applied Research in Education, *A Survival Guide for the Preschool Teacher* (1991) and *Complete Handbook of Indoor and Outdoor Games and Activities for Young Children* (1994), as well as the author of *Kids' Atlanta* and other materials for teachers. She is married and is the mother of two children and two dogs.

ABOUT THIS BOOK

When you think of science, do you think of a rocket scientist, a thick textbook, abstract facts, or complicated experiments? Science for young children couldn't be further from these assumptions. The purpose of this book is to make science come alive in your classroom with fun, simple, meaningful activites for children. And the best part is that I'm not a rocket scientist, but an early childhood teacher just like you! I took the challenge of writing this book for children because they love science. They are fascinated by the world in which they live, their bodies, and all the phenomena they experience every day. Science is also important because it "invites" children to think and use their minds.

SCIENCE SURPRISES! is a treasure of over 200 fun and exciting ideas. Each activity suggests a major theme area and skills which are enhanced. The materials are safe and simple—most of which you can find in your kitchen or playground. There are step-by-step directions and helpful illustrations, as well as challenging follow-up activities and simple explanations. The major sections are:

Science Center Sensations—Suggestions for setting up a science center, as well as materials, tools, and games that will encourage exploration.

Exciting Experiments—Just like "magic," these experimetns spark children's interest, questioning, and problem solving skills.

Disccovery Boxes—This chapter presents science boxes that you can create for independent or small group learning or take-home activities.

Nature Club—Take learning out on the playground and into your community with fun explorations that build children's respect and love for all living things.

Earth Day, Every Day—Help children become sensitive to ecological problems and how they can help the environment.

Artful Expressions—Science and art are a "natural" combination with these creative activities that encourage "process" rather than "product" art.

Edible Science—Children cook, eat, and learn as science concepts are reinforced.

Weaving Science Across the Curriculum—Integrate science into all areas of the classroom from math and reading to music and movement.

Growing Together—Parents and children have fun learning and growing together with the many activities that can be copied and sent home.

Resources From A to Z—Where to order materials, how to set up field trips or obtain guest speakers, and children's literature are a few of the many ideas you'll find in this chapter.

You'll find that the activities, experiments and recipes in SCIENCE SURPRISES! will challenge children and open the door to those magic moments of discovery. Enjoy them with your children!

Jean R. Feldman

INTRODUCTION

Sciences is SURPRISES! It's doing, exploring, thinking, talking, sharing, and playing—all things children do naturally and well! The world is full of wonderful things from worms on the sidewalk and "pictures" in the clouds, to giant bubbles and popcorn seeds. The activities and materials in this book offer you an opportunity to share all these wonderful "surprises" and magic moments of discovery with children.

Why Is Science Important for Children?

Science provides the perfect vehicle for children to learn as they play and explore. Children are innately curious about the world in which they live, and science gives them some insight into understanding their world and themselves. Science sharpens children's senses and contributes to their total development, including language, motor skills, social interaction, intellectual skills, and emotional development. Science also provides a meaningful web for integrating math, reading, and other goals in your curriculum. Further, through science children are able to develop lifelong skills of observing, problem solving, questioning, experimenting, and exploring. Above all, science nurtures a love and respect for our world and all living things.

How Do Children Learn Science?

Children don't think abstractly and can't learn science through lectures and reproducible handouts. Children do learn through their senses, and therefore need active experiences with hands-on materials in order to construct their own knowledge. Activities also need to be open-ended to enable all children to experience success and to accommodate their different styles of learning.

It's important to think of science as a process, rather than a product. From preschool through graduate school, these same steps of discovery will guide learning:

- *Observing*—Children's interest is sparked and they use their senses to take in data. By seeing, hearing, smelling, tasting, and touching, they begin to construct knowledge about objects and events. Teachers can help children by focusing their attention on little things.

- *Classifying*—Children attempt to sort and categorize that information on the basis of some property or attribute. (Remember that there are different ways to group objects.)

- *Questioning*—Children raise questions about "What would happen if...?" or "I wonder why...?"

- *Measuring*—Children use quantifying skills (counting, measuring, comparing, estimating) as they observe and investigate.

- *Predicting*—Children make predictions about what might happen based on their past experiences. Children should be encouraged to make "hypotheses, or educated guesses, of what the outcome will be.

- *Experimenting*—Children make their predictions after investigating and freely exploring materials. Child-directed experiments where it's O.K. to make mistakes should be provided.

- *Communicating*—As children describe their experiences and what they see it helps clarify their thinking. It also gives the teacher the opportunity to introduce vocabulary and supportive information. Children enjoy sharing their discoveries with classmates or can record information with journals, drawings, graphs, videos, and other media.

- *Researching*—Children learn how to find out more information by looking in books and magazines, going to the library, or consulting experts.

Where Do Children Learn Science?

Science must be" experienced" by children, which suggests we provide them with a multitude of different materials and learning environments. A science center provides a safe place for children to investigate independently in an open-ended way. They have the freedom to manipulate and explore in their own style, and have the leisure to continuously repeat experiments. Also, in a science center with challenging tools and interesting objects, children can choose to study what is of particular interest to them.

Experiments with the class or small groups of children offer another technique for learning. Cooperative learning and class projects give children the opportunity to work as a community. Field trips, guest speakers, films, and stories are yet other ways children can develop science concepts.

And what more "natural" place to do science than on your playground and in your community? Plants, rock formations, weather, animals, and other natural wonders await eager young scientists in all seasons of the year.

Science should not be isolated, but integrated throughout the day and year. Reading stories about animals, building volcanoes in the sandbox, writing letters to politicians about environmental problems, counting the legs on a spider, buying fruit at the market, planting a garden on the playground, and painting with sticks and leaves are all examples of how science can be an exciting part of other content areas.

Just as the timing of a rainbow or when a butterfly will burst into flight cannot be predicted, when and where children learn science cannot always be predicted. Finding a turtle on the way to school or ice in a bucket on the playground can be the trigger for a science unit. Therefore, science should not be based solely on what the teacher "thinks" children should learn, but should reflect the children's interests and natural curiosity. Being sensitive to children and following their lead can evolve into meaningful learning and contribute to an "emergent" curriculum.

What Is the Role of the Teacher?

Adults can't really "teach" children science, but can facilitate and nurture their learning in many ways. Following the suggestions below, you can create a science program that is alive, fun, and a journey of discovery for you and your children.

1. Establish a learning environment where children feel safe to take risks and make mistakes. Respect everyone's thoughts and efforts, and focus on the process of learning rather than a specific outcome.

2. Build a sense of community in your classroom where children can work together to solve problems and explore new objects. Science should be a social time where children talk to each other and share ideas.

3. Be flexible and sensitive to children's special interests and styles of learning. Simplify or add steps to make the activities appropriate for all children.

4. Provide children with many interesting objects to explore and give them science tools they can investigate with. Rotate materials frequently to maintain their attention.

5. Offer children choices with a variety of activities they can do alone, in a small group, or with the entire class.

6. Answer children's questions if you can, but don't be afraid to say, "I don't know." Show them how to find additional information by looking in books or going to the library.

7. Plan for long periods of uninterrupted time for children to be involved in science activities.

8. Set limits for children so they will feel secure and have some boundaries for their explorations.

9. Teach children how to care for equipment and clean up after their experiments.

10. Conduct frequent safety checks to make sure materials and equipment are in good condition. (Supervise children carefully with certain tools and experiments.)

11. Take advantage of the "teachable moment" and try to extend learning in other content areas. Help children connect information and see relationships in their daily lives.

12. Create a child-centered program by listening to children and following their lead.

13. Coach children with support, suggestions, and additional information, and cheer them with a smile, hug, or word of encouragement.

14. Model the steps in the scientific process for children and become actively involved in learning with them.

15. Reflect their enthusiasm and excitement over the little things in our world.

In addition to the strategies above, use open-ended questions to develop critical thinking skills. Too often teachers ask" yes" or "no" questions, or those that require a single word. Open-ended questions will encourage children to think critically, make comparisons, make predictions, and synthesize information. Questions similar to the ones below will expand thinking skills and language:

How are _____and _____ alike? How are they different? Why do you think that _____? What would happen if _____?

Accept divergent answers and avoid putting a value judgment on children's responses. Instead of evaluating what they say, simply repeat their idea. Also, make sure you give them ample time to respond.

Finally, make science FUN so children will develop positive attitudes and want to keep learning and growing.

CONTENTS

I

Science Center Sensations

Hands-On Science

Discovery Zone

CAUTION Young Scientists at Work!

The science center, or "discovery zone," will be an exciting area where children can touch, hear, see, smell, and taste. Interesting objects, books, tools, and classroom pets will spark children's curiosity and give them the opportunity to investigate, experiment, and learn on their own level and in their own unique way.

Setting Up a Science Center

The purpose of the science center is to provide children with a special area where they can actively learn and discover either independently or in a small group. Interesting and unusual objects will draw children like a magnet, hands-on materials will invite them to explore, and tools and open-ended activities will encourage them to experiment.

Follow these suggestions for a "sensational" science center:

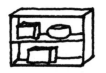

- Place the science center near a window so there will be plenty of light for growing plants.

- A sink or water table nearby will be useful for many experiments.

- Use a bookshelf for displaying collections, resource books, and science magazines.

- Lunchroom trays, clear tubs, plastic ziplock bags, detergent boxes, and shoe boxes can all be used to store materials and collections.

- Label all materials with the word and a picture clue.

- Keep classroom pets, an aquarium, ant farm, or terrarium in the science center to encourage observation.

- A bulletin board will be useful for displaying posters, pictures, and newspaper or magazine articles. Language experience stories of nature walks or rebus directions of experiments can also be posted on the bulletin board.

- Provide children with a rug or table and chairs so they can sit down comfortably and become involved with the materials.

- Rotate collections and materials frequently to keep children's interest. Provide objects that relate to the season, unit of study, or an area of interest expressed by the children.

- Encourage children to bring their own collections or "treasures" they find at home. Let them share items they find on the playground or on nature walks in the science center.

- Give children ample time to explore in the science center. They will often want to do experiments continuously to verify their results.

- Teach children how to use science materials properly. Give them the responsibility for caring for classroom pets and plants.

- Provide children with developmentally appropriate materials and tools so they may successfully play and learn.

Science Center

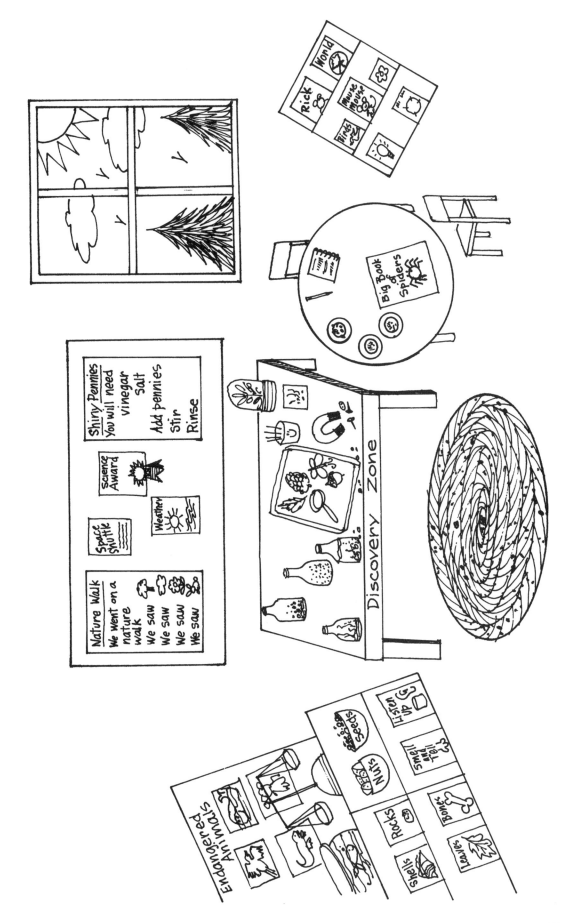

Permanent materials in your science area might include:

magnifying glass

mirror

large stool magnifier

magnets

balance scale

thermometer

flashlight

stethoscope

color paddles

kaleidoscope

books, encyclopedia

prism

science magazines

classroom pets

plants

aquarium

terrarium

ant farm

Rotate these collections or seasonal objects to create interest:

rocks

seeds

shells

leaves, pine needles, cones

feathers

nuts

animal bones

flowers

bird nest

"feely" cards

sand or soil samples

smelling jars

water samples

photographers

simple machines

models

dead insects

hearing aid, prosthesis, and other tools of people with special needs

Remember, when you are excited about experiments and natural objects, children will reflect your enthusiasm. Spend time with them in the science center, model how to use the equipment, ask questions, listen to their discoveries, and value their joy and confidence from learning about their world.

COLOR WINDOWS

Theme: colors; senses (seeing)

Skills: experimenting; observing; communicating

Materials: 6 paper plates

clear acetate or cellophane in red, yellow, and blue (clear report folders work well)

scissors

stapler

Directions:

1. Using the paper plate as a pattern, trace circles on the acetate or cellophane and cut them out.

2. Cut the centers out of the plates, leaving the rim.

3. Place each colored circle between two plate rims and staple in place.

4. Let the children look through the color windows to see how the world changes colors. Encourage them to describe what they see.

5. Ask children to put two plates together and describe what happens.

Challenges:

Take the color windows outside and let the children experiment.

Let children mix colored water together to make new colors, or let them mix up their own paints to make new colors.

Tape colored acetate to the windows in your classroom for the children to look through.

Do the color dance. Cut out 3″ circles of red, yellow, and blue acetate. Give each child a circle, then put on some music for them to dance to. When the music stops, the children must match up their circle with a circle of a different color to make a new color. Continue starting and stopping the music as the children make new colors.

Explanation: The three primary colors are red, yellow, and blue. They can be combined to make the secondary colors of orange, purple, and green.

red + blue = purple

red + yellow = orange

yellow + blue = green

SMELL AND TELL

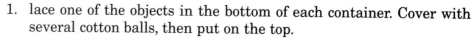

Theme: senses (smelling)

Skills: classifying; inferring

Materials: 6 film containers

cotton balls

objects with distinguishing smells, such as coffee,

oregano, peppermint, chocolate, peanut butter,

baby powder, bubble gum, cinnamon, and so on

Directions:
1. lace one of the objects in the bottom of each container. Cover with several cotton balls, then put on the top.
2. Let the children take off the top, smell, and try to identify what is in the container.
3. Which one smells good? Is there one that you dislike?

Challenges:

Have the children smell the containers, then ask them to wet the end of their noses by licking their fingers and touching them. Can they smell better when their noses are wet? Have they ever felt an animal's nose that was wet? Can animals smell better than people?

Take index cards and draw a picture clue of the objects in the containers on the cards. Ask the children to match up the pictures to the odors.

Make two containers of each smell, then ask children to match up like smells.

Give children a snack and tell them to hold their noses and eat it. Can they taste it? Why not? Can they taste things as well when they have a cold?

Go on a nature walk and smell various plants and objects. Do they all smell the same?

Explanation: Our noses help us smell and identify objects by their odors.

© 1995 by The Center for Applied Research in Education

FUNNY FEELINGS

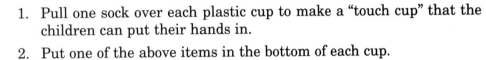

Theme: senses (touching); nature

Skills: classifying; inferring; communicating

Materials:
5 large plastic cups

5 old socks

2 of each of the following: rocks, sticks, shells, leaves, nuts

Directions:
1. Pull one sock over each plastic cup to make a "touch cup" that the children can put their hands in.
2. Put one of the above items in the bottom of each cup.
3. Display the other items on a tray or in a box lid.
4. Children feel the object in each cup, then match it with an object from the tray.
5. Encourage the children to describe the objects in the cups.

Challenges:
Use leaves of different shapes, different kinds of rocks, different types of flowers, and so forth.

Have children identify and match up spoons, crayons, soap, blocks, toys, and other common objects.

Let children sit at a table, take off their shoes, and try to identify different objects with their feet.

Explanation:
Nerves in our hands and other parts of our body send messages to the brain to help us identify what we feel.

TOUCH BOOKS

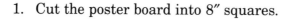

Theme: senses (touching)

Skills: exploring; communicating

Materials:

poster board

2 book rings

scissors, hole punch, glue

various textures, such as cotton, sandpaper, bubble wrap, contact paper (sticky side), corrugated cardboard, satin, and so on

Directions:

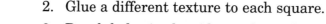

1. Cut the poster board into 8″ squares.
2. Glue a different texture to each square.
3. Punch holes in the sides and put the pages together with the book rings or pipe cleaners.
4. Encourage the children to touch the pages and describe how they feel. Which one feels best? Which one feels rough? Smooth?
5. How could you feel these if you didn't have hands? Let the children rub the textures with different parts of their bodies.

Challenges:

Tape different textures to the floor, then let the children take off their shoes and feel them with their feet.

Go on a discovery walk outside and identify how different objects feel.

Give children a variety of objects and ask them to sort them by how they feel.

Ask children to bring in an object from home that they like to touch.

Let children make their own touch books, or let them make a collage of different textures.

Explanation:

There are nerves in our hands and other parts of our bodies that let us touch things and send messages to our brain about how they feel.

SOUND MATCH

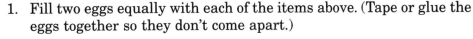

Theme: senses (hearing)

Skill: classifying

Materials: 12 plastic eggs
egg carton
rice, beans, salt, paper clips, buttons, cotton balls, basket or box

Directions:

1. Fill two eggs equally with each of the items above. (Tape or glue the eggs together so they don't come apart.)
2. Put the eggs in a basket, then let the children shake the eggs until they find two that make the same sound. Have them put matching eggs side by side in the egg carton.
3. Continue matching eggs until the carton is full.

Challenges:

Ask children to guess what they think is inside the eggs.

Play a game by passing the eggs out to the children. Let them move around shaking their eggs until they find one that makes a similar sound.

Use film containers instead of plastic eggs to make this game.

Hide a music box or portable radio in the room or out on the playground and ask the children to try and locate where the sound is coming from.

Explanation: Our ears pick up sound waves and help us identify noises we hear.

WATER SCOPE

Theme: senses (seeing); water

Skills: observing; experimenting

Materials: plastic food container (cottage cheese, yogurt)
clear plastic wrap
rubber band
scissors
water

Directions:

1. Cut the bottom out of the food container.
2. Loosely cover the hole with plastic wrap and rubber band in place. Gently push down in the center of the wrap to make a shallow indentation. Fill with a small amount of water.
3. Place the water scope over small leaves, flowers, rocks shells, and other classroom objects and observe what happens. Why?
4. How is a water scope like a magnifying glass? How is it different?

Challenges:

Play with the water scope on the playground.

Make a water scope to use in the water play table or when you go to the beach. Cover the container tightly with the plastic wrap and rubber band in place. Use it to look down in the water.

Fill a clear jar with water and screw on the lid tightly. Look at objects through it. What happens?

Get a glass of water and put a pencil in it. What happens to the pencil? Why?

A large water scope can be made with a plastic ice cream gallon. Cut two circles in the sides that your hand can fit through. Cover the top with plastic wrap, rubber band in place, and fill with water. Let the children stick their hands in the holes to observe different objects.

Explanation: Water acts as a lens, bending the light rays so that objects appear larger.

© 1995 by The Center for Applied Research in Education

BALANCE SCALE

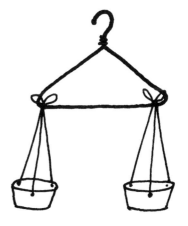

Theme: math (measurement)

Skills: measuring; comparing; predicting

Materials:
coat hanger
2 margarine tubs
yarn or string
hole punch
tape, ruler

Directions:
1. Punch three evenly spaced holes in the sides of the margarine tubs.
2. Tie an 18″ piece of string to each hole.
3. Bring the ends of the strings together, knot, then tie the ends to the hanger as shown.
4. Tape the ruler down on a table so that the end extends out approximately 8″.
5. Place the hanger on the ruler.
6. Let the children put blocks, crayons, play dough, and other classroom objects in the tubs and compare them. Are they the same (equal)? Which has more? Which has less?
7. Ask children to select two objects, predict which is heavier, then verify their guesses by placing them on the balance scale.

Challenges: Bring in a bathroom scale, kitchen scale, and other tools used for weighing objects.

Explanation: A scale is a tool used to measure the weight (mass) of an object.

FUNNEL PHONE

Themes: sound; telephones; senses; (hearing)

Skills: communicating; experimenting

Materials: 2 plastic funnels
4′ to 8′ of plastic tubing 3/8″ thick (available at hardware stores)
tape

Directions:
1. Fit each end of the plastic tubing in one of the funnels and tape in place.
2. Have one child hold a funnel to his/her ear while another child talks in the other funnel.
3. How does the sound travel from one funnel to the next?

Challenges: Get a piece of string, 2 cups, and 2 paper clips. Poke holes in the bottom of each cup, thread an end of the string through, and tie a paper clip to the end of the string. Take turns talking and listening in the cups.

Attach a long piece of plastic tubing to a fence or piece of playground equipment to make a similar telephone.

Explanation: Sound travels in sound waves through the plastic tubing and is magnified by the funnel on the end.

© 1995 by The Center for Applied Research in Education

MIRROR PLAY

Themes: senses (seeing); mirrors

Skills: experimenting; observing

Materials: small mirror

paper

magazines

scissors

glue

Directions:

1. Cut out small pictures from the magazine and cut them in half.
2. Glue one half of each picture to a sheet of paper.
3. Let the children take the mirror and place it next to the pictures. What happens? Why does it look like the whole picture again?

Challenges:

Ask the children to write their names, then hold the mirror next to them. Can they write their names so they look correct in the mirror?

Have children draw their own designs and half-pictures to reflect in the mirror.

How many different things do we use mirrors for?

Tape three small mirrors together to make a triangle. Place an object in the middle and observe how it is reflected in the mirrors.

Explanation: Mirrors reflect the image of light that is shown in them.

PERISCOPE

Themes: senses (seeing); mirrors

Skills: observing; experimenting

Materials: two 3″ square mirrors (available at craft stores)
milk carton (quart size)
utility knife
masking tape

Directions:

1. Using the grid shown below, draw lines on opposite sides of the carton at the top and at the bottom.
2. Cut slits along these lines with the utility knife.
3. Cut a 1″ square in the top and bottom on opposite sides of the carton as shown.

Side 1   **Side 2**   **Side 3**   **Side 4**

4. Insert the mirrors in the slits so they face each other and reflect off each other.
5. Tape the sides to hold the mirrors in place and protect the sharp edges.
6. Let the children experiment with the periscope inside and outside on the playground.

Explanation: With a periscope, the two mirrors are angled to reflect light from an object twice so the object is not seen directly.

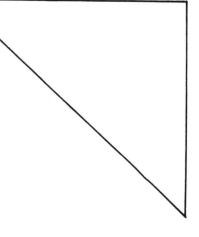

FLASHLIGHT FUN

Themes: light; color

Skills: experimenting; observing

Materials:
flashlight
batteries
cellophane (red, yellow, blue)
rubber bands
black paper

© 1995 by The Center for Applied Research in Education

Directions:

1. Let the children play with the flashlight. Ask them to take it apart and put it back together.

2. Give children different colors of cellophane to wrap around the flashlight, securing in place with a rubber band. What happens to the light? What happens when you put blue and yellow cellophane together? Red and blue? Red and yellow?

3. What happens when you cover the flashlight with black paper? Trace around the end of the flashlight on black paper. Cut small shapes out of the circle, then tape it to the flashlight. What happens when you shine it on a white piece of paper?

Challenges: Give children different kinds of flashlights to play with.

Use the flashlight to play "I Spy." Turn off the lights in the room and ask children to find an object of a particular color, shape, or beginning with a certain sound.

Explanation: Some objects are transparent and light will shine through them; other objects are opaque and light cannot go through them.

MAGNETIC CHALLENGE

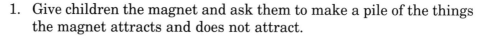

Theme: magnets

Skills: experimenting; predicting

Materials: *magnet

plastic bottle with screw-on lid

objects that a magnet will attract and will not attract (paper clips, safety pins, tissues, scissors, plastic toys, erasers, nails, blocks, pencils, pens, and so on)

Directions:

1. Give children the magnet and ask them to make a pile of the things the magnet attracts and does not attract.
2. How are the things the magnet attracts alike?
3. Let the children go around the room and hunt for other objects that the magnet will attract.

Challenges:

Put a paper clip in a cup of water. Will the magnet pick it up through the water?

Place a paper clip on top of a piece of cardboard. Put the magnet under the cardboard and try to move the paper clip.

Scatter paper clips or iron filings in the sand table, then let the children use magnets to attract them.

Fill a plastic bottle halfway with sand. Put paper clips, pins, nails, and other small metal objects in the bottle and screw on the top. Shake the bottle to cover the objects. Give the children a magnet to "find" the objects in the bottle.

Explanation: Magnets attract objects made from steel or iron.

© 1995 by The Center for Applied Research in Education

---

*Caution children not to take magnets near computers. (With younger children, you might want to tie the magnet to a string so it stays in the science area.)

SHELL SEEKERS

Themes: ocean; shells

Skills: exploring; classifying; researching

Materials: collection of shells
magnifying glass
book of shells
small pail

Directions:

1. Place the shells in the pail and encourage the children to explore them by feeling them, listening to them, using the magnifying glass, and so on.
2. Let the children sort the shells by shape, color, size, and other attributes.
3. Give the children the shell book and ask them to match up the shells with the pictures of the shells in the book.
4. Read additional information about the shells and the animals who once lived in them.

Challenges: What other animals have shells? Why do some animals need shells?

How about a hermit crab for a classroom pet?

Do rubbings of the shells by laying a piece of paper on the top and gently rubbing with the side of a crayon.

Play with the shells in the water table. Do they sink or float? Why?

Make a mosaic by gluing small shells to a heavy sheet of paper. Make a necklace by stringing shells with holes on a piece of string or yarn.

Explanation: Some animals live in shells, then discard them when they outgrow them or die.

BOTTLES OF FUN

Themes: water; ocean; sink and float

Skill: observing

Materials:

plastic bottles with lids   crayon shavings
glitter   sand, small shells
plastic bottles with lids   white corn syrup
food coloring   beads, buttons, small trinkets
dirt   vegetable oil
dishwashing liquid

© 1995 by The Center for Applied Research in Education

Directions:

1. Fill one bottle with water, then add a few drops of food coloring and some glitter. Shake it up or hold it up to the light.

2. Put several spoonfuls of dirt in the bottom of a bottle then fill it to the top with water. Shake it up to make muddy water, then watch as the dirt settles to the bottom.

3. Fill a bottle halfway with water. Add a drop of detergent and a drop of food coloring. Put on the top, then shake it and make bubbles.

4. Add crayon shavings to a bottle of water.

5. Fill a bottle with 1/2 cup of corn syrup and several drops of food coloring. Move it around slowly to coat the sides.

6. Put a layer of water, vegetable oil, and corn syrup in a bottle. Add buttons, beads, or plastic trinkets and observe which one sinks to the bottom first.

7. Put some sand in the bottom of a bottle, then add some shells, water, and blue food coloring.

8. Fill a bottle with 2/3 of water. Add a few drops of food coloring, then fill it to the top with vegetable oil.

Challenge: Let children make their own bottles and fill them with liquids and objects of their choice.

Explanation: The density of various liquids is different and causes objects to float and sink at different rates.

Hint: Glue the tops of the bottles on with tile and grout glue to prevent spills.

18

TORNADO IN A BOTTLE

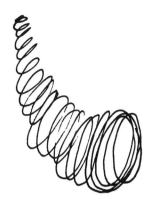

Themes: weather; tornadoes; wind

Skill: observing

Materials:
plastic bottle with a flat bottom
water
food coloring
liquid detergent
marble

Directions:

1. Fill the bottle 3/4 full with water. Add a drop of food coloring and a drop of detergent.
2. Put the marble in and screw on the lid tightly.
3. Swirl the bottle around in a circular motion and you will create a "tornado" (vortex) in the bottle.

Challenges:

Tear up little pieces of foil and styrofoam and add "trash" to the tornado bottle.

Let children spin around like a tornado.

Practice emergency procedures for a tornado warning.

Explanation:

A tornado is a very strong wind that blows in a spiral or vortex and is shaped like a funnel. In nature tornadoes form where cold air flows into a region of warm air.

STAR GAZER

Themes: stars; night

Skill: observing

Materials: oatmeal canister or cylinder from chips
hammer
nail

Directions:

1. Draw the points of a constellation on the bottom of the can.
2. With the hammer and nail, punch holes in all the points.
3. Cut out a small eye hole in the lid.
4. Hold the can up to a light and look through the hole to view the constellation.
5. Decorate the outside of the can and label it with the name of the constellation.

Challenges:

Make several star gazers of different constellations.

Let children match up illustrations of constellations with appropriate cans.

Give children a black sheet of paper and let them punch holes with a push pin or pencil. Place the paper on an overhead projector to simulate stars at night.

Explanation:

The stars in the sky were used as a navigation device in earlier times, for example, the north star. People often imagined figures (constellations) in the sky.

CRYSTAL COLLECTION

Themes: crystals; rocks

Skills: observing; classifying

Materials:
strong magnifying glass
rock salt
table salt
rock sugar
sand
rocks containing crystal formations (quartz, mica, gems)
tweezers
black paper

Directions:

1. Let the children observe the various crystals with a magnifying glass on the dark paper.

2. How are the crystals like? Can you see the flat sides (faces)? Count the flat sides on the crystals. Do they have the same number?

Challenge:

Take a dark sheet of paper outside on a cold, snowy day and try to catch snowflakes and observe them with a magnifying glass to see the crystals.

Explanation: Crystals have particular shapes formed by flat surfaces that meet to make angles.

SEEDS AND PACKETS

Themes: plants; seeds

Skills: classifying; predicting

Materials: 6–8 packets of seeds (pumpkin, radish, sunflower, popcorn, watermelon, cucumber, beans, carrots)
poster board
glue
scissors

Directions:

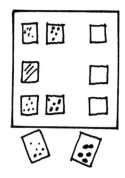

1. Cut the poster board in half.
2. Cut 3″ squares from one half. Glue several seeds from each packet on a square.
3. Glue the seed packets to the other piece of poster board.
4. Let the children match up the seeds to the packets they came from.

Challenges:

Plant the remaining seeds in a classroom garden or let the children each plant their own in a paper cup.

Get a seed catalog and match up seeds with pictures.

Sort birdseed or mixed beans.

Explanation: Some plants produce seeds that will grow into new plants.

TERRARIUM

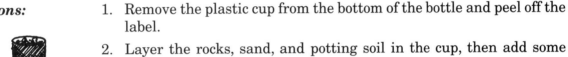

Themes: plants; rain forest

Skills: experimenting; observing

Materials: 2 liter soda bottle with plastic cup at the bottom

small pebbles or gravel

sand

potting soil

small plants and moss

Directions:

1. Remove the plastic cup from the bottom of the bottle and peel off the label.
2. Layer the rocks, sand, and potting soil in the cup, then add some small plants and moss. (A shell or small toy figure is also fun to add.)
3. Take the top of the bottle and cut it off as shown. (You can use this as a funnel.)
4. Cut two slits in the bottom of the bottle, then insert it over the terrarium to make a dome.
5. Water the terrarium and set it where it will receive sunlight. (If it "fogs up" remove the top for a few hours. If it gets too dry, then add more water.)

Challenges: How is the rain forest like a terrarium?

Take two clear plastic cups and layer gravel, sand, and soil in the bottom of one. Add a plant and water it. Put the second cup on top and tape where the cups join to make a terrarium.

Explanation: A terrarium is like a habitat with its own supply of light, water, and food.

WORM FARM

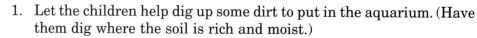

Themes: earthworms; habitats

Skills: observing; communicating

Materials: aquarium or large, clear jar

shovels and pails

soil

earthworms

leaves, shredded carrots, lettuce leaves, and other bits of garbage

Directions:

1. Let the children help dig up some dirt to put in the aquarium. (Have them dig where the soil is rich and moist.)

2. Look under logs and rocks for worms to add to the "worm farm." A good time to look for worms is after it rains. (If you need help, go to a store that sells fishing bait and buy worms.)

3. After placing the worms in the aquarium, add a layer of decaying leaves to the top. Keep in a cool, dark place, and cover with a towel.

4. Add fresh leaves and humus daily, and mist with water. Place shredded carrots, lettuce leaves, and other fruits and vegetables on top and observe to see which ones the worms prefer.

5. Have the children look at the worms through the sides of the aquarium, or allow them to gently pick up the worms if they want to. (Remind children to wash their hands after holding the worms.) How do the earthworms feel? How do they move?

6. Return the worms to where you found them after a week or two of study.

Challenges: Cover the sides of the aquarium with black paper for several days, then remove the paper to see the tunnels.

Find out how earthworms help the soil.

Draw pictures of the worms and write the stories about them.

Play with plastic fishing worms in the sand table.

Add caterpillars, tadpoles, snails, hermit crabs, or other animals to your science center.

Explanation: Like other animals, earthworms need space, shelter, food, and water.

© 1995 by The Center for Applied Research in Education

PET SHOP

Themes: pets; animals

Skills: communicating; classifying

Materials: empty pet food boxes and containers
                    collars, pet toys, brushes, cages, dishes, and so on
                    pictures of animals or stuffed animals

Directions: 1. Discuss the different characteristics of pets, including how to care
                       for them, feed them, clean them, and so forth.

                    2. Let the children sort the food, toys, grooming supplies, cages, and
                       other items with the appropriate pictures or stuffed animals.

Challenges: Ask the children to draw pictures of their pets or to bring photographs
                    from home.

                    Let children take turns bringing their pets for show and tell. (Some can
                    stay all day, while others will need to be taken home.)

                    Do a graph of the children's favorite pets.

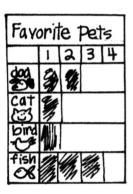

                    Create a pet shop or veterinarian's office in the dramatic play area. Let
                    the children decorate cardboard boxes for cages and bring in stuffed
                    animals from home to play with.

                    Play "Guess Who I Am?" as children take turns acting out different pets
                    while their friends guess what they are.

Explanation: Pets have different kinds of foods, toys, cages, and needs.

ANIMAL HOMES PUZZLE

Themes: animals; homes; habitats

Skills: classifying; communicating

Materials: poster board
                  scissors
                  glue
                  pictures of animals and their homes (see following page)

Directions: 1. Cut the poster board in 6″ × 3″ rectangles.
                  2. Glue matching animals and their homes on the rectangles, then cut between the pictures in puzzle shapes.

                  3. Mix up the pictures, then let the children match up appropriate pictures. (This will be a self-checking activity.) Encourage the children to name the animals and their homes.

Challenges: Go on a nature walk and look for animal homes.

                  Ask questions such as, "Why doesn't a bear live in a nest in the tree?" "Why doesn't a hamster live in a doghouse?" Why does a spider live in a web?"

                  Have children draw or paint pictures of animals and their homes.

                  Make a similar puzzle game where children match up mother and baby animals, or animals and their products. (Old workbooks often have good pictures you can use.)

Explanation: Animals need different kinds of homes to live in.

© 1995 by The Center for Applied Research in Education

DOES IT FIT?

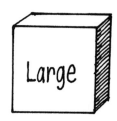

Themes: math; sizes

Skills: predicting; comparing

Materials:

3 boxes: large (cardboard box); medium (shoebox); small (jewelry box)

variety of classroom objects and items from the science center (crayon, shell, rock, block, pencil, book, ball, doll, truck, and so forth)

Directions:

1. Label each of the boxes "large," "medium," or "small."

2. Let the children take each object, predict which box it will fit in, then place the object in the box to test their predictions.

3. Ask children to name other objects that would fit in each box, or let them sort pictures of objects into appropriate boxes.

Challenges:

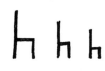

Tell the story of the "Three Bears," and let the children match up flannel board pictures of the bear's bowls, chairs, and beds. Children could also build appropriate beds and chairs for the bears in the block area.

Have children sort pictures of objects that are bigger and small than them.

Get food containers (boxes, bottles, and cans) that are empty and wrap them in black paper. Let children guess what kind of food came in each container.

Explanation:

Objects do not change shape and will only fit in containers that are larger than they are.

© 1995 by The Center for Applied Research in Education

HAVE A HABITAT

Themes: animals; habitats, homes

Skill: classifying

Materials:
pictures of animals (science magazines, stickers, or children's drawings)
construction paper
scissors, glue
poster board
crayons or markers
cloth tape

Directions:
1. Cut out animal pictures and glue them to 4″ × 6″ pieces of construction paper or index cards.
2. Cut 3 pieces of poster board that are 8″ × 11″. On one sheet print "water" and draw a symbol for water. On a second sheet print "land" and draw a symbol for land. On the third sheet write "air" and draw a symbol for air.
3. Tape three sheets together at the sides and set them on the floor or table as shown.

4. Ask children to sort the pictures according to where each animal lives.

Challenges:
What do all animals need to live?
Which animals live on the land? In the water?
Let children paint a mural depicting land, water, and air animals.

Explanation:
All animals have a habitat that meets their needs for shelter, food, and water.

SORT IT OUT

Themes: nature; homes

Skills: classifying; predicting

Materials: 2 boxes
magazines
marker
scissors

Directions: 1. Label one box "inside" and the other box "outside." (Add a picture clue to the labels.)

2. Ask the children to cut out magazine pictures of objects they could find inside their home or outside in nature, such as a bed, car, tree, refrigerator, swing, dish, and so forth.

3. Have the children sort the pictures into the appropriate box.

Challenges: What objects can be found inside and outside?

Make other sorting games to use with the boxes, such as clothes you wear in the winter and summer; things that are living and nonliving; objects that are big and little; things you like and dislike.

Explanation: Objects can be classified as to where they are commonly found.

WEATHER CHART AND SONG

Themes: weather; clothing

Skills: communicating; predicting

Materials: paper plate
                     markers or crayons
                     brad fastener
                     construction paper scraps
                     yarn, hole punch, scissors

Directions:

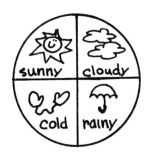

1. Divide the paper plate into fourths and decorate it with weather symbols similar to the one below. (Adapt the weather symbols to the climate in your part of the country.)
2. Make an arrow from the construction paper and attach it to the middle of the plate with a brad fastener.
3. Punch a hole in the top and tie on a piece of yarn for a hanger.
4. Sing the weather song below each day as one child puts the arrow on the appropriate weather picture.

Weather Song (Tune: Bingo)

There is some weather in the sky
And Windy is its name-o.
W-I-N-D-Y, W-I-N-D-Y, W-I-N-D-Y,
And Windy is its name-o.

Change the words of the song to "Sunny," "Rainy," "Snowy," or "Cloudy" to match the weather.

Challenges: Encourage the children to choose the clothing they will need for the expected weather.

Invite a meteorologist to talk to your class, and bring in weather articles and forecasts from the paper.

Explanation: Weather changes according to the atmospheric changes in pressure, temperature, moisture, and the season.

GUESS AND DRAW

Themes: nature; senses

Skills: predicting; communicating

Materials:
gift box with a lid
ribbon
paper, crayons, pencils
object from nature (rock, seed, shell, pine cone, and so on)

Directions:

1. Each day put a different object in the box. (Tie it up with a ribbon so the children won't be tempted to take a peek!)
2. Put the box in the science center, along with paper, crayons, and pencils. Challenge the children to shake the box and guess what is inside.
3. Ask the children to draw a picture of what they think it is. (Older children can write a sentence about what the mystery object is.)
4. At the end of the day, encourage the children to talk about their predictions, then open the box to reveal the mystery object.

Challenges:

Let the children have turns taking home the box and filling it with a natural object. Have them give clues as their friends try to guess what it is at circle time.

Take a clear container and fill it each day with different natural objects. Let the children estimate how many objects are in the jar, then empty the contents and count together.

Explanation: We can use our senses to help us determine what an object is, even though we can't see it.

SCIENCE HANG-UPS

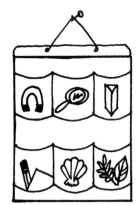

Theme: nature

Skills: observing; sorting; classifying; exploring

Materials: shoe rack (one with pockets that hangs on a door)

magnifying glass

magnet

prism

paper and pencil

flashlight

natural objects (shells, leaves, flowers, feathers, nuts, seeds, bones, rocks, nest, dead insects, animal skins, and so forth)

Directions:
1. Hang the shoe rack in the science center from a wall or the back of a shelf.
2. Fill each compartment with one of the above materials.
3. Children can take out the different objects and explore them.

Challenges: Use the shoe rack for a sorting activity. Let children sort nuts, feathers, shells, and other objects.

Create collections in the shoe rack that relate to a unit of study. You might fill it with different kinds of leaves, rocks, or bark.

Explanation: Objects in our world can be classified and sorted according to like characteristics—size, weight, type.

SCIENTISTS' TOOLS

Themes: science tools; scientists and engineers

Skill: communicating

Materials:

    plastic beakers and test tubes
    funnels
    petrie dishes
    magnifying glass or microscope
    tongs
    science journals and magazines, books
    safety goggles
    lab coat
    eye dropper
    calculator
    magnet
    balance scale
    notebook and pencil

pictures of various scientists (include pictures of men and women of different ethnic groups)

Directions:
1. Display the pictures of the different scientists in the science center.
2. Let the children play with the tools and materials scientists use.

Challenges: Put the science tools in the dramatic play center and create a "lab."

Invite parents who are involved in different science professions to come and talk to the class. Ask them to include information on how they prepared for their careers. What they like best about their jobs, and what made them decide to become scientists or engineers.

Ask children to draw a picture or write a story about what kind of scientist or engineer they might like to be when they grow up.

Put funnels, eye droppers, test tubes, and beakers in the water table.

Explanation: There are many different interesting and rewarding careers in science and engineering fields.

II

Exciting Experiments

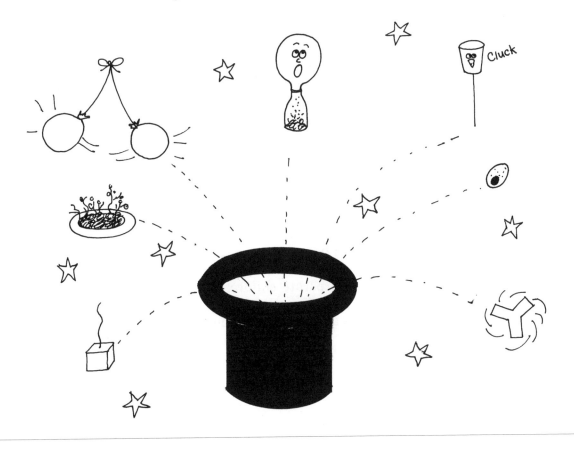

Science experiments are like "magic" to children and will ignite their curiosity and thinking skills. By observing, predicting, and communicating results, children really are "scientists." Be open to their suggestions and explanations, and involve them as much as possible with hands-on experiences. And remember that it's okay to make mistakes. There is no such thing as an experiment that "doesn't work," because there is always something to be learned!

Ready—Set—Go
(Suggestions for Exciting Experiments)

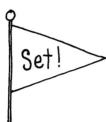

Collect all materials and equipment you will need before you begin. (Involve the children in the preparation, as well as the clean-up.) Cover the floor with newspaper if necessary, and have plenty of paper towels on hand.

Think the experiment through to make sure you have everything you could possibly need.

Have children sit comfortably on the floor or around a table before you begin. If possible, conduct experiments with small groups of children to allow more participation and interaction. Arrange materials so all children can easily see what's going on. Explain what materials you have and the steps you will follow. Print directions on a language experience chart to encourage reading skills.

Let children smell, feel, shake, use their senses, and explore individual items you will be using. Ask open-ended questions that will stimulate critical thinking skills and predictions. For example, "What do you think will happen if _____? Why _____? Does anybody else have an idea about what might happen?" (Avoid putting value judgments on children's hypotheses by simply repeating what they say.) Accept as many ideas and explanations as children offer.

Conduct the experiment, challenging children to observe carefully. Follow up experiments by asking children to tell you what happened. Again, use open-ended questions so children can use words to describe what they have seen and what they are thinking. Questions such as, "Why do you think that . . . ?" "How did . . . ?" "What made . . . ?" and "I wonder why . . . ?" will enable children to work out their own explanations. Often children will want to repeat experiments to verify results, and they should be encouraged to do so. As children observe an experiment a second time, their competence and confidence are increased. Also, try to incorporate children's input on how to change or extend experiments when you repeat them. Conclude experiments with resource books and suggestions on how they can learn more.

IT'S A GAS!

Themes: chemical reaction; gas

Skills: experimenting; communicating

Materials: drink bottle

vinegar

baking soda

large balloon

marker

pie pan

spoon

Directions:

1. Blow up the balloon several times to stretch and loosen it up.

2. Draw a silly face on the balloon with a marker. Pour several spoonfuls of baking soda into the balloon. (You may need to use a funnel to do this.)

3. Place the drink bottle in the pie pan and fill it with 1/2 cup of vinegar.

4. Insert the balloon over the mouth of the bottle, tip the bottle over, and observe what happens when the baking soda and vinegar mix. What makes the balloon blow up?

5. Ask the children to describe what happened, or let them draw pictures of the experiment.

Challenge: Pour a package of yeast into a drink bottle. Add 1/2 cup of warm water and 1 tbs. of sugar and gently swirl the bottle around until the yeast dissolves. Insert a balloon over the mouth of the bottle and observe what happens to the balloon over the next 15 minutes.

Explanation: Mixing soda with vinegar causes a chemical reaction that releases carbon dioxide gas. The gas expands and takes up more space, causing the balloon to inflate.

VOLCANIC ACTION

Themes: volcanoes; chemical reaction

Skills: observing; experimenting

Materials:
tall cup
tray or tub
sand or gravel
vinegar
food coloring (red)
baking soda

Directions:

1. Place the cup, mouth up, in the middle of the tray and build up around it with wet sand or gravel to form a mountain with a hole in the top.
2. Pour 1 cup of vinegar in the cup and add a few drops of red food coloring.
3. Stir in 1/4 cup of baking soda and watch the volcano erupt.

Challenges:

How is this like a real volcano? How is it different?

What causes a real volcano? Go to the library and find out.

Look on the globe to see where volcanoes have erupted on the earth over the past several years.

Explanation: Volcanoes erupt when the molten lava from the hot interior of the earth comes up through the earth's surface due to an eruption underground.

POP AND FIZZ

Themes: air; gas; buoyancy

Skills: observing; experimenting

Materials: popcorn kernels
Alka-seltzer tablets
tall glass

Directions:

1. Fill the glass with water.
2. Drop 10 popcorn kernels in the glass, then add the Alka-seltzer tablets.
3. Watch what happens to the popcorn kernels. What makes them go up and down in the glass?

Challenge: Drop several small raisins in a glass of ginger ale or clear soda and watch them bob up and down.

Explanation: The Alka-seltzer makes gas bubbles that collect around the kernels, making them light so they float to the top. When the kernels reach the surface the bubbles pop, so the kernels sink to the bottom again.

PENNY POLISH

Theme: chemical reaction

Skills: experimenting; observing

Materials: old, dirty pennies
vinegar
salt
lemon juice
soapy water
3 plastic bowls
spoons
paper towels

Directions:

1. Mix 1/2 cup vinegar and 1 tbsp. salt in one bowl.
2. Pour 1/2 cup of lemon juice in the second bowl.
3. Prepare soapy water in the third bowl.
4. Ask the children to predict which solution will polish the pennies the best.
5. Let them take one penny at a time and stir it in a bowl to determine which one cleans the best.
6. Remove the pennies and dry them off. Was their prediction correct?

Challenge: Can you clean other coins with the same solution?

Explanation: The copper penny becomes darker as it oxidizes in the air. The chemicals in the vinegar and salt cause the copper oxide coating to dissolve and reveal a new shiny layer of copper.

PEPPY PEPPER

Themes: water; friction

Skills: experimenting; observing

Materials: bowl of water
pepper
liquid detergent

Directions: 1. Sprinkle pepper on the top of the water.
2. Squirt a drop of detergent in the middle of the bowl.
3. Where does the pepper go? Why?

Challenges: Try a similar experiment using baby powder instead of pepper.

Float some toothpicks in a bowl of water, then touch a bar of soap to the middle and observe what happens.

Explanation: Detergent reduces the surface tension on water surface in the middle of the bowl and the pepper is drawn by the stronger surface tension at the edge of the bowl. Surface tension occurs on a free liquid surface as a result of the natural attraction between water molecules.

QUAKING QUARTER

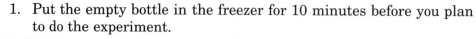

Themes: heat; energy

Skills: experimenting; observing

Materials: quarter
glass bottle (with mouth the size of a quarter)
cup of water

Directions:

1. Put the empty bottle in the freezer for 10 minutes before you plan to do the experiment.

2. Take out the cold bottle and dip the mouth in the water., Then dip the quarter in the water and place it on the mouth of the bottle. The water acts as a seal around the edge of the quarter.

3. Put your hands around the bottle and hold them still.

4. The quarter should wiggle and "quake."

Challenges: Blow up a balloon to stretch it. Put a glass bottle in the freezer for 10 minute, then insert the balloon over the mouth of the bottle. Stick the bottle in a pan of hot water and watch the balloon inflate.

What happens to the lid on a pot of water when the water begins to boil? Why?

Explanation: The heat from your hands warms the air in the bottle and causes it to expand. As the air expands, it lifts the quarter slightly and some air escapes around its edges, out of the bottle causing the quarter to move.

© 1995 by The Center for Applied Research in Education

RUBBER EGG

Themes: chemical changes; eggs

Skills: experimenting; observing

Materials:
clear jar with lid
vinegar
raw egg in its shell

Directions:

1. Put a raw egg in a jar, then cover it with vinegar. Talk about how the vinegar smells. Screw the lid on the jar and set it aside for 3–5 days.

2. Have the children observe the egg each day and describe what is happening to it.

3. After 3–5 days, the egg shell should be almost invisible. Remove the egg, rinse it off, and hold it up to the light. How does the shell feel? Hold the egg several inches from the table and drop it. Does it break?

Challenges:

Soak a hard boiled egg in vinegar for several days then feel the shell. Drop it. What happens?

How can you tell a raw egg from a hard boiled egg? Try to spin both eggs. The hard boiled egg should spin, while the raw egg will fall over.

Clean raw chicken bones, then soak them in vinegar for 24 hours. They should be pliable like rubber and can be bent into different shapes.

Explanation: The vinegar dissolves some minerals from the eggshell, making the shell soft.

FLOATING EGG

Themes: salt water; sink and float

Skills: experimenting; predicting

Materials: clear glass or bowl

salt

spoon

egg

Directions:

1. Fill the glass with water. Ask if the egg will sink or float if you put it in the glass.
2. Gently drop the egg in the water and observe what happens.
3. Remove the egg and stir in 2 tbsp. of salt. Drop the egg in the glass again and observe what happens.
4. Continue adding 2 tbsp. of salt to the water and stirring until the egg floats. How many tablespoons did it take?
5. Why do you think the egg floats in salt water?

Challenge: Is it easier to float in the ocean or in a fresh water lake? Why?

Explanation: The density of water is increased when salt is added, so the egg floats in the salt water because it is denser.

© 1995 by The Center for Applied Research in Education

COLOR SWIRL

Themes: colors; chemical changes

Skills: experimenting; observing

Materials: pie pan

whole milk

food coloring

liquid detergent (*"Dawn"* works best)

Directions:

1. Pour 1 cup of milk in the pie pan and let it sit at room temperature for one hour.
2. Add several drops of food coloring to the sides of the pan at different intervals.
3. Squirt a drop of the detergent in the middle of the pan and observe the colors as they swirl around. (You might have to wait a few seconds or jiggle the pan a little to get the colors moving.)

Challenge: Try this experiment with skim milk. Will it work?

Explanation: The detergent causes the cream to separate and makes the colors swirl.

GOOP

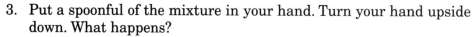

Themes: liquids; solids

Skill: experimenting

Materials: cornstarch
water
spoon
bowl

Directions:

1. Pour 1 cup of cornstarch in the bowl.
2. Slowly add 1/2 cup water and stir until the mixture is the consistency of thick gravy. (You may need to add a little more water to get it the right consistency.)
3. Put a spoonful of the mixture in your hand. Turn your hand upside down. What happens?
4. How is it like a liquid? How is it like a solid?

Challenges: What's the difference between liquids and solids? Make a separate list of objects that are solids and liquids.

Add food coloring to the goop.

Let the children mix their own goop in a plastic cup.

Pour several boxes of cornstarch in the water table and let the children add water and make a giant glob of goop!

CRYSTAL GARDEN

Theme: *crystals

Skills: experimenting; observing

Materials: aluminum pie pan or baby food jar

                    charcoal

                    table salt

                    **clear ammonia

                    water

                    laundry bluing

                    food coloring

                    bowl and spoon

Directions: 1. Mix 2 tbsp. salt, 1 tbsp. ammonia, 2 tbsp. water, and 2 tbsp. bluing together

                    2. Place the charcoal in the pie pan or jar, then pour the above mixture over it. Sprinkle several drops of food coloring on top.

                    3. Set the pan in a quiet place where it can be observed but won't be disturbed.

Challenge: How long does it take the crystals to grow? How long will they last?

Explanation: Crystals may be formed when a substance is dissolved in a liquid, and the liquid then evaporates.

© 1995 by The Center for Applied Research in Education

---

*Supervise this experiment carefully as these crystals could be harmful to children.

**Adults will need to do this as ammonia is dangerous for children to handle.

CRYSTAL CANDY

Theme: crystals

Skills: experimenting; observing

Materials: sugar

water

tall jar or glass

pan, spoon, stove

pencil

string

paper clip

Directions:

1. Mix 2 cups of sugar and 1 cup of water in the pan. Bring to a boil and continue boiling for one minute until it reaches the "soft boil" stage (242°F on a candy thermometer).
2. Cool slightly, then pour the mixture in a tall glass or jar.
3. Tie a piece of string that's as long as the jar to a pencil, then tie a paper clip to the other end of the string.
4. Suspend the string in the water mixture and observe it for several days. it should form rock candy crystals that you can eat. (Leave the jar still so the can form.)

Challenges: Look at sugar and salt crystals with a magnifying glass.

Add food coloring to the sugar mixture and see what happens.

Explanation: Crystals can be formed when a solid crystalline substance is dissolved in a hot liquid and then cools and solidifies. Hot water can dissolve and keep more sugar in solution.

AIR, AIR, EVERYWHERE

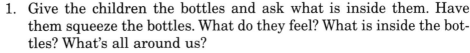

Theme: air

Skills: experimenting; observing

Materials: plastic bottles (different sizes and shapes)
                cardboard rollers from toilet paper

Directions:

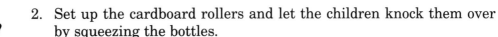

1. Give the children the bottles and ask what is inside them. Have them squeeze the bottles. What do they feel? What is inside the bottles? What's all around us?
2. Set up the cardboard rollers and let the children knock them over by squeezing the bottles.
3. How is wind like the air in the bottles? Can you see the wind? How can you tell if it's blowing?

Challenges: Play with the bottles in the water table. What comes out of them when you squeeze them under water?

Challenge children to move plastic boats and toys with the air in the bottles.

Blow up balloons, then release them. What causes them to fly around the room?

Get a party blower and a plastic bag. Blow air into the bag as you hold it in your fist. Insert the end of the party blower in the bag and tape it in place. Squeeze the bag to make the blower unfurl, then release the bag.

Explanation: Moving air is called wind. When you squeeze the bottle, it pushes the air outside and creates wind.

WHIRLY COPTER

Themes: flying objects; air

Skill: experimenting

Materials: paper

                              scissors

                              paper clip:

Directions:

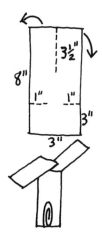

1. Cut a piece of paper that is 8 1/2″ × 3″.
2. Cut a slit down the middle that is 3 1/2″ long.
3. Come up 3″ from the opposite end and cut a 1″ slit in each side as shown.
4. Bend in the bottom sides to overlap and put a paper clip in the end.
5. Fold top flaps at a slight angle in opposite directions to make the rotor blades.
6. Hold the whirly bird up in the air, then let it go and watch it spin.

Challenges: Decorate your copter with markers or crayons.

                              Play with whirly copters out on the playground.

Explanation: The air passing under the rotor blades causes the copter to rotate and to float down.

PING-PONG-PING

Theme: air

Skills: experimenting; observing

Materials: hair dryer
                      ping-pong ball

Directions: 1. Turn on the hair dryer, then center the ping-pong ball where the air comes out. Observe what happens to the ball.
                      2. Slowly move the dryer from side to side, observing the ball as you do so.
                      3. Why does the ping-pong ball seem to follow the hair dryer? What happens when you turn the dryer off?

Challenge: Experiment with small pieces of paper and other objects to see if the air from the dryer will suspend them.

Explanation: The air current keeps the ball aloft and equalizes the air around the ball, causing it to follow the dryer when you move it.

PARACHUTE

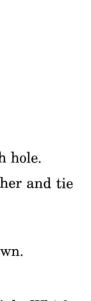

Themes: air; flying objects

Skills: experimenting; observing

Materials: string

plastic bag (from laundry) or light fabric

plastic spool or small toy

Directions:

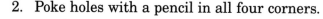

1. Cut a 12″ square from the plastic or cloth.

2. Poke holes with a pencil in all four corners.

3. Cut four pieces of string 14″ long and tie one end in each hole.

4. Lay the parachute flat, then bring all four strings together and tie in a knot where they meet.

5. Tie a spoon or small toy to the knot.

6. Throw the parachute up in the air and watch it glide down.

Challenges: Make parachutes of different sizes from a variety of materials. Which works best? Why?

Play with parachutes out on the playground.

Explanation: The amount of air under the parachute causes it to float to the ground slowly.

BALLOON ROCKET

Themes: rockets; air

Skills: experimenting; observing

Materials:
straw
string (20′ long)
*large balloon
tape

Directions:
1. Thread the string through the straw.
2. Tie the string to opposite sides of the room. (You can tie the string to chairs, a bookshelf, window, flag pole, and so on.)
3. Blow up the balloon, holding the end tightly so no air escapes.
4. Tape the inflated balloon to the straw.
5. Let the end of the balloon go and watch it zoom to the other end of the room. What makes it fly?

Challenge: Give children balloons they can blow up and let go out on the playground.

Explanation: As the pressurized air escapes from the balloon it creates a thrust that pushes the balloon forward.

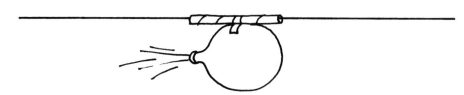

*Balloons need to be carefully supervised as younger children can choke on them.

BOOMERANGGGGGG!

Themes: air; flying objects

Skill: experimenting

Materials: heavy paper (tagboard or file folders work well)
scissors

Directions:

1. Trace around the pattern on the following page on tagboard and cut it out.
2. Practice throwing the boomerang so it will come back to you.

   Hint: Hold it at your waist and gently fling it up and away from you with a flick of your wrist.

Challenges: Decorate boomerangs with markers or crayons.

Try different types of paper to see which one works best.

What letter does the boomerang look alike?

Bring in a real boomerang from Australia and compare it with the paper one. Find out how boomerangs were used by the bush tribes of Australia.

Explanation: The shape of the boomerang, along with the air under it, enables it to fly back to you.

Boomerang Pattern
(Cut from heavy paper or tagboard.)

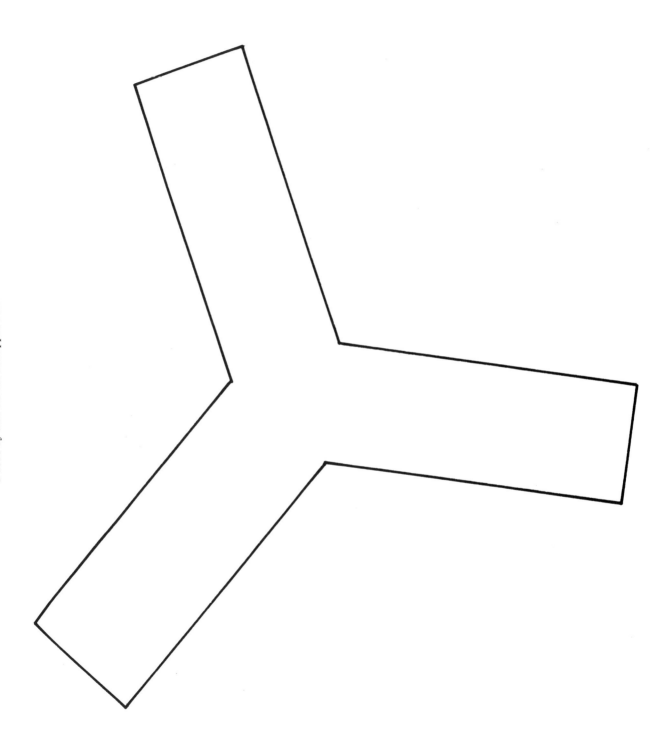

MAKE A RAINBOW

Themes: colors; rainbows

Skills: experimenting; observing

Materials: clear glass
mirror
sunny window

Directions:
1. Fill the glass with water and place it in a sunny window.
2. Place the mirror in the glass at an angle.
3. Turn the glass around until you make a rainbow on the ceiling or wall.
4. What colors do you see in the rainbow? (Hold up a white piece of paper to the rainbow so you can see all the colors.)

Challenges: Make a rainbow outside with the hose on a sunny day.
Get a prism and make rainbows with it.

Explanation: The mirror and water break down the light into the color spectrum. ROY G. BIV will help you remember the colors in the rainbow—R-Red, O-Orange, Y-Yellow, G-Green, B-Blue, I-Indigo, V-Violet.

REFLECTORS

Theme: light

Skills: experimenting; observing

Materials: cardboard scraps
aluminum foil
scissors

Directions:

1. Cut rectangles from the cardboard that are $4'' \times 6''$.
2. Cover the rectangles with aluminum foil. (Make sure to put the shiny side out.)
3. Go outside and hold the reflector in the sun. Can you make the sun reflect from the card?

Challenges:

Try this experiment on a cloudy day. Will it work? Why not?

Put the card in the sun. How does it feel? Why? Put the card in the shade. Now how does it feel? Why?

Explanation: The aluminum foil acts as a mirror and reflects light.

ME AND MY SHADOW

Themes: shadows; light

Skills: observing; predicting

Materials: film projector or overhead projector

screen or large sheet of white paper

toys and classroom objects

Directions:

1. Set up the film projector so it shines on the screen or white paper.

2. Choose one object at a time to hold in front of the light to make a shadow on the wall. Ask the children to predict which object made the shadow.

3. Let children make shadows with their hands and arms. What causes shadows?

Challenges:

Trace around each child's silhouette, then play a guessing game to identify who it is.

Make shadow puppets to use in dramatizing a story.

Play shadow tag out on the playground.

Give children a flashlight to make shadows with.

Explanation: When the source of light is blocked, a shadow of the object is made.

NOW YOU SEE IT—NOW YOU DON'T!

Themes: light; senses (seeing)

Skill: observing

Materials: clear glass
sticker or stamp

Directions:

1. Fill the glass half full with water. Place it on the top of the sticker.
2. Observe the sticker by looking by looking down at it through the water.
3. Observe the sticker through the side of the glass. Where did it go? Did it disappear?
4. Once again observe the sticker from the top of the glass.

Challenge: Put a penny or other small object under a glass of water and make it disappear.

Explanation: The reflection of light through the glass gives the optical illusion that the sticker has disappeared.

LONG AND SHORT OF IT

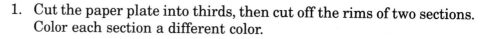

Theme: senses (seeing)

Skill: observing

Materials:
paper plate
crayons
scissors

Directions:

1. Cut the paper plate into thirds, then cut off the rims of two sections. Color each section a different color.

2. Place the rims on top of each other to make sure they are equal.

3. Place one rim under the other. Which one looks longer? Which one looks shorter? Why?

4. Reverse the position of the rims. Do they look the same now?

Challenges:

Do similar experiments with pencils and straws by placing them at different angles and observing how they appear to be different lengths.

Make balls of equal amounts of clay. Are they the same amount? Roll one into a pancake and ask if they're the same amount.

Explanation:

Optical illusions are created when the longer arch is next to the shorter one, causing it to look longer.

© 1995 by The Center for Applied Research in Education

EVAPORATION

Themes: water; evaporation

Skills: experimenting; observing

Materials: paper towels

water

Directions:

1. Give each child a wet paper towel.
2. How long will it take to dry the paper towel? What can they do to make them dry faster?
3. Let children experiment to see who can dry their paper towels first.
4. Where did the water in the paper towels go?

Challenges:

Try this experiment outside on the playground.

Let children paint invisible pictures. Give them each a cotton swab, a cup of water, and a paper towel. Have them paint with the water on the paper towel., then ask them where their pictures went.

Put equal amounts of water in both a pie pan and glass. Which will evaporate faster? Why?

Mix sugar water and salt water. Put each solution in a pie pan and set in a sunny window. What happens when the liquid evaporates? Taste the crystals left in the pan.

Explanation: Wind and heat cause water to evaporate in the air more quickly. Warm air holds more water vapor than cold air.

CLUCKER

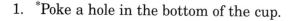

Themes: birds; senses (hearing)

Skills: experimenting; communicating

Materials:
plastic cup

cotton string

paper clip

scissors

water

Directions:
1. *Poke a hole in the bottom of the cup.
2. Cut a piece of string 18″ long and thread it through the hole in the bottom of the cup.
3. Tie the paper clip to the end of the string in the cup.
4. Hold the cup in one hand, and pull down on the string with the index finger and thumb on the other hand. What happens?
5. Wet the string, then pull down on it. Pull in jerky movements to make a clucking sound. Why does it make a noise when you wet it?

Challenges:
Decorate the outside of the cup to look like a chicken or turkey.

Sing "Old MacDonald," making the clucking noise when you get to "on his farm he had some chicks."

How are a guitar and violin like the clucker?

Explanation:
The water creates friction on the string, which vibrates in the cup to create a sound.

---

*An adult will need to do this with scissors or a hammer and nail.

© 1995 by The Center for Applied Research in Education

RAIN IN A JAR

Themes: rain; weather

Skills: observing; predicting

Materials:
glass jar with a lid

hot water

ice cubes

Directions:
1. Fill the jar half full with hot water. Put it in a warm spot, then put several ice cubes on top.

2. Observe the jar for several minutes. What makes it "rain" in the jar?

3. What do you think happens when the warm air on the earth hits the cold air in the sky?

Challenges:

Hold a pie pan over a pan of steaming water. Observe what happens when the steam hits the pie pan. Why does it "rain" in the pan?

Wet a sponge, then seal it in a ziplock baggie. Hang it in a sunny window and watch it "rain" in the bag.

What happens to the outside of a glass or aluminum can when you have a cold drink on a hot day? How is it like the rain in the jar?

Explanation:
As the warm moist air near the earth's surface rises and hits the cold air in the clouds, it condenses and makes it rain. Warm air can hold more water vapor than cold air.

WATER TRICK

Themes: air; water

Skills: experimenting; observing

Materials: glass
water
paper towel
paper plate
sink or tub

Directions:
1. Fill the glass with water.
2. Fold the paper towel in half and put it on the plate. Place the plate and towel upside down on the glass.
3. Hold the glass in one hand, pressing the plate against the glass with the other hand as you turn it upside down. (Do this over a sink or tub.)
4. Slowly remove your hand from the plate. Taa daa! (The water should stay in the glass upside down for several seconds.)

Challenges: Try this trick with a square of cardboard or other heavy paper.

Place a straw in a glass of water. Put your finger over the top of the straw, then remove it from the glass. Why does the water stay in the straw?

Explanation: The pressure of the air outside the glass is greater than the pressure of the water inside.

ICE ON A STRING

Themes: ice; evaporation

Skills: experimenting; observing

Materials: ice cube

salt

spoon

paper plate

8″ piece of string

Directions:

1. Place the ice cube on the paper plate.

2. Wet one end of the string and lay it on the ice cube. Try to lift the ice cube with it. What happens?

3. Sprinkle a spoonful of salt over the string. Wait a minute or two, then try to lift the ice cube with the string. What happens? Why?

Challenges:

Why do people put salt on icy sidewalks in the winter?

Freeze a large block of ice in a plastic bowl. Remove it and pour warm water over it. Sprinkle salt and food coloring on top and observe what happens.

Explanation: Salt lowers the freezing temperature, so the ice melts around the string. However, after a few minutes the ice refreezes around the string because the freezing point rises again.

DISSOLVE SOLVE

Theme: dissolving

Skills: experimenting; predicting

Materials:

water   oil

spoons   styrofoam pieces

10 cups   ice cube

sugar   powdered drink mix

salt   small pieces of paper

pepper   laundry detergent

sand

Directions:

1. Fill the cups with water.
2. Ask the children to predict if the different objects will dissolve in the water.
3. Let them add a different item to each cup and stir it. What happens? Were their predictions correct?

Challenge: Take a glass of hot water and a glass of cold water. Add a spoonful of powdered drink mix to each and observe. (Do not stir!) Why does the mix dissolve faster in the hot water?

Explanation: Some materials break down in water, while others do not. Hot water has a greater capacity to dissolve and hold substances in solution than cold water.

© 1995 by The Center for Applied Research in Education

ABSORPTION

Theme: absorption

Skills: experimenting; predicting

Materials:

cup of water	paper towel
eye dropper	toothpicks
tray	construction paper
aluminum foil	plastic bag
cotton ball	cardboard
wax paper	paper towel
facial tissue	wooden block
piece of fabric	styrofoam plate
plastic plate	cork
sponge	spoon (metal)

Directions:

1. One by one, let the children place the above items on the tray. Ask them if they think the objects will absorb the water.

2. Give them the eye dropper and have them drop water on the objects to test their predictions.

3. Ask the children to sort the objects that absorb and do not absorb the water.

Challenges: Conduct this experiment on the playground to determine which objects in nature absorb water.

Put petroleum jelly on your hand, then run it under water. What happens? Why?

Take 5 toothpicks and bend them in half, but do not break them apart. Arrange them to make a star with ten points. Put a drop of water in the middle, then observe the toothpicks as they "move" to make a five-pointed star.

Explanation: Some objects are more porous and will absorb liquids.

LAYERED LIQUIDS

Theme: liquids

Skill: observing

Materials: plastic bottle

vegetable oil

white corn syrup

water

Directions:

1. Fill the bottle 1/3 full with corn syrup.

2. Add 1/3 water, then fill to the top with vegetable oil.

3. Observe the liquids. Slowly turn the bottle around and upside down. Why don't the liquids mix? Which one is always on the top? Which one is always on the bottom?

Challenges:

Drop a small bead in the bottle. Does it float through all the liquids the same?

Pour some vegetable oil in a clear jar, then add a few drops of food coloring. Why doesn't the food coloring mix with the oil?

Explanation:

The syrup is denser than the oil and water, so it sinks to the bottom. The oil is least dense, so it floats on top.

© 1995 by The Center for Applied Research in Education

MELT DOWN

Theme: heat

Skills: experiemnting; predicting

Materials:
muffin pan

marshmallow

crayon

chocolate chip

block

cotton ball

ice cube

pencil

scissors

plastic toy

hot, sunny day

Directions:

1. What happens if you have an ice cream cone and you set it outside on a hot day? Why does it melt? What other objects will melt in the hot sun?

2. Place the objects above in the muffin pan, along with other items the children suggest. Make a list of the objects the children think will melt.

3. Place the pan in the hot sun for one hour, then compare what happens with the children's predictions. Why do some things melt in the sun?

Challenges:

Freeze water in small plastic cups. Give each child a cup and see who can melt theirs the fastest.

Color water with red, yellow, and blue food coloring, then pour it in ice cube trays and freeze. Place 2 different colored cubes in plastic baggies and zip shut. What happens when the ice cubes melt? what secondary colors are formed?

Explanation: Some materials melt when they are heated.

FRICTION STICKS

Themes: friction; energy

Skills: experimenting; predicting

Materials: 2 sticks
block
mitten

Directions:

1. Ask the children to describe the temperature of their hands. Have them place their hands on their cheeks to feel them.
2. Have them briskly rub their hands together. Ask how their hands feel now. What made them warm?
3. Give each child two sticks to rub together quickly. How do they feel after they are rubbed? Why?
4. Get a block and rub it against the carpet quickly. How does it feel?
5. Let children predict how a mitten and other common items will feel when they are rubbed. What makes them warm?

Challenges: Slide your feet quickly on the rug, then feel the bottoms of your soles.

What happens when you go down a slide very fast?

Explanation: When things are rubbed together they create friction, and the energy of the rubbing motion causes heat.

STRAW STRENGTH

Themes: energy; motion

Skills: experimenting; observing

Materials: large potato
plastic straw

Directions:

1. Give one child a straw and the potato. Ask if they think the straw is strong enough to poke a hole through the potato, then let them try to do so. (The straw should bend, making it difficult.)

2. Give another child the potato and straw. Instruct them to put their index finger on top of the straw and hold it high in the air. Have them hold the potato in their other hand and stick it out in front of them. Tell them to quickly bring down the straw with their finger in top. Taa daa! The straw should go through the potato.

3. Why could the straw pierce the potato the second time?

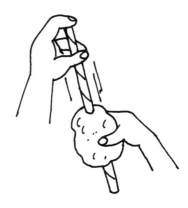

Challenge: Try a similar experiment with a straw and an apple.

Explanation: Since no air can escape the straw with your finger on top, the compressed air in the straw strengthens it so it can pierce the potato.

WHEELS FOR WORK

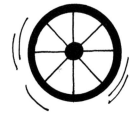

Themes: simple machines; wheels

Skills: experimenting; communicating

Materials: wagon or other riding toy

Directions:

1. Have two children stand up. Tell one child to move the other child across the room. Is it easy?
2. Ask one child to sit in the wagon, then have the other child push the wagon across the room. Why is it easier?
3. Let children try to move other objects across the room by pushing them or moving them in the wagon.
4. How do wheels make our life easier?

Challenges:

Brainstorm all the ways we use wheels.

Let children make a "wheel" mural by cutting out pictures or drawing objects with wheels.

Paint with wheels. Dip the wheels of toy cars in paint, then "drive" them across paper

Explanation: A wheel is a simple machine that makes work easier.

STATIC BOX

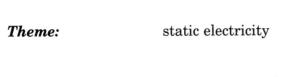

Theme: static electricity

Skills: experimenting; observing

Materials: stationery or notecard box with a clear plastic lid

                   tissue paper

Directions: 1. Cut or tear the tissue paper into small pieces (1/2″)and put them in the bottom of the box.
                   2. Put the lid on the box and rub across rapidly with the palm of your hand.
                   3. What happens to the tissue paper? Why?

Challenges: Put styrofoam packing, newspaper strips, pieces of a plastic bag, and other objects in the box to see what happens. Try using pennies or buttons. What happens? Why?

                   Shuffle your feet across carpeting on a cold, dry day, then touch a metal doorknob. Did you get a shock? Turn off the lights and observe the spark when you touch the doorknob. How is the spark like lightning?

                   Shuffle your feet across the floor and touch a friend. What happens if you touch a wooden object first? Lick your finger before touching the doorknob and see what happens.

Explanation: Static electricity is created when you rub the top of the box, causing the pieces of paper to repel each other and be attracted to the lid of the box.

SALT AND PEPPER

Themes: static electricity

Skills: experimenting; observing

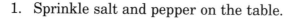

Materials:
salt

pepper

comb

Directions:

1. Sprinkle salt and pepper on the table.
2. Take the comb and run it over the salt and pepper.
3. Now take the comb and briskly brush it through your hair 25 times.
4. Run the comb over the salt and pepper and observe what happens. Why is the pepper attracted to the comb?

Challenges:

Blow up two balloons. Tie each one to a piece of string that is 18″ long. Rub each balloon against a wool sweater, then hold the ends of the string together in the air. Why do the balloons repel each other?

Cut a paper doll out of newspaper and attempt to stick it to the wall. Rub the side of a pencil quickly over the paper doll, then hold it up to the wall.

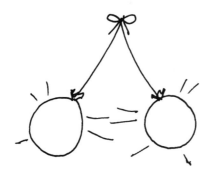

Explanation: Brushing the comb through the hair gives it a negative charge, so the pepper is attracted to it.

© 1995 by The Center for Applied Research in Education

MAKE A MAGNET

Theme: magnets

Skills: experimenting; observing

Materials: 2″ nail
strong magnet
pins, paper clips

Directions:

1. Challenge the children to pick up a pin or paper clip with the nail. Does it attract the object?
2. Rub the nail 50-100 times in one direction with the magnet, then try to pick up pins or paper clips. What happens? Why?
3. How did the nail get magnetized?

Challenges:

Will the nail pick up heavier objects? If you stroke it more times will it get stronger? What happens if the nail sits for a day?

Give children several different kinds of magnets (bar, horseshoe, refrigerator) and let them find objects that the magnets will attract. How are the objects alike?

Let children play with magnets and metal objects in the water table. Will the magnet attract through water?

Hide iron fillings or paper clips in the sandbox for children to find with a magnet.

Explanation:

Rubbing the nail in one direction causes the atoms to line up and attract certain objects.

GRAVITY

Themes: gravity; weight

Skills: experimenting; observing

Materials: thick book and thin book
big block and small block
pencil and eraser
large stuffed animal and small animal

Directions:
1. One at a time let a child stand on a table or chair. Hand the child two of the above objects and ask which one is heavier. Which one is lighter?
2. Ask the class which one they think will land first if they are both dropped at the same time. Why?
3. Let the child drop the objects as the others observe what happens. Were their predictions correct? Why did the objects land at the same time?
4. Continue letting other children stand up and drop different pairs of objects.

Challenge: Crumple up a sheet of paper and hold it in one hand. Hold a plain sheet of paper in the other hand and let them go at the same time. Why didn't gravity have the same pull on them?

What would the earth be like without gravity? Why is there no gravity in space?

Explanation: Gravity is the force that pulls objects toward the earth.

© 1995 by The Center for Applied Research in Education

INVISIBLE PLANTS

Themes: plants; mold

Skills: experimenting; observing

Materials: roll, muffin, or piece of brown bread

ziplock bag

magnifying glass

Directions:

1. Have the children pass the bread around the room.
2. Sprinkle the bread with water, then seal it in the bag. Place the bag in a dark corner of the room.
3. Observe the bread as the mold grows. Look at the mold with a magnifying glass.
4. Where did the mold come from? How did it get into the bag?

Challenges:

How are molds helpful? (Used to make some medicines.) How are molds harmful? (Can cause allergies and spoil food.)

Grow some yeast. Fill a cup with warm water, then stir in a tbsp. of sugar and a package of yeast. Observe the yeast as it grows. What foods are made with yeast?

Explanation: Mold is an invisible plant that is in the air.

GROWING JELLY BEANS

Themes: seeds; plants

Skills: experimenting; predicting

Materials:
5 clear cups

potting soil

jelly beans

lima beans

pennies

popcorn kernels

candy corn

Directions:

1. Have the children recall experiences of planting seeds and growing things. If you plant a flower seed, will you get a tomato? Why not? If you plant a pencil, will you get a pencil tree? Why not?

2. Have the children fill the cups with potting soil. Show them the jelly beans, lima beans, pennies, popcorn kernels, and candy corn. Let them predict which ones will grow.

3. Plant the above objects in the cups.(Place them next to the sides of the cups so the children can observe them as they grow.)

4. Put the cups in a sunny window and water.

5. Encourage the children to observe the cups daily and describe what they see.

6. Which things grew? Why? Which things did not grow? Why?

Challenge: Have the children go on a "seed hunt" in their kitchens and yards to find seeds to plant. Label the seeds and keep a journal of the ones that grow.

Explanation: Seeds grow into the same kind of plant they come from.

© 1995 by The Center for Applied Research in Education

BABY BEANS

Themes: seeds; plants

Skills: observing; communicating

Materials:
dry lima beans
paper towels
plastic bag
paper and pencils

Directions:
1. Place the lima beans between paper towels and wet them thoroughly.
2. Put the beans in the plastic bag, seal and set in a warm place overnight.
3. Let the children dissect the beans the next day. (Demonstrate how to take the seed coat off, then gently separate to see a little plant.)
4. Ask the children to draw pictures of the beans and the "baby plants" inside them.

Challenges: Soak other dry beans and dissect them.

Grow lima beans in a plastic bag. Fold a paper towel to fit in a sandwich bag. Staple halfway across the bag. Put in several dry lima beans, water, fold over the top, and staple to a bulletin board. Observe to see how long it takes for the stem and root to appear.

Explanation: Seeds contain "baby plants" or embryos that will grow into new plants.

GROWING, GROWING EVERYWHERE

Themes: plants; seeds

Skills: experimenting; observing

Materials: cotton balls

styrofoam egg carton

sponge

pine cone

corncob

baking potato

soil

birdseed, grass seed, or other seeds

spray bottle, pie pans

Directions:

1. Place a cotton ball in each section of the egg carton. Water the cotton balls, then sprinkle them with different seeds. Keep moist daily with a spray bottle.
2. Soak the sponge, corncob, and pine cone in water. Place them in the pie pan, then sprinkle with seeds. keep moist with the spray bottle.
3. Hollow out the baking potato and fill it with dirt. Plant some seeds in it and water.

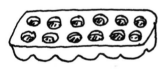

Challenge: Take a nature walk and look for plans that are growing in unusual places, such as moss on a rock or vines on a fence.

Explanation: Seeds can grow in many different places, where they have moisture and warmth.

HAIRY HEAD

Themes: plants; seeds

Skills: experimenting; observing

Materials:
plain paper cups
potting soil
grass seed (rye works best)
markers
scissors

Directions:

1. Let the children draw faces on their cups with markers.
2. Fill the cups half full with soil, then sprinkle grass seed on top.
3. Water the seeds, then set the cups in a sunny window.
4. Make a graph to see how long it takes the grass to grow.
5. When the "hair" in the cup gets too long, cut with scissors.

Challenges:

Take an eggshell and draw a face on it. Fill with soil and plant grass seed in it.

Experiment to see what it takes to make the seeds grow. Put one cup in a dark closet, don't water one, and don't use soil in another. What happens?

Explanation: Seeds need soil, sun, and water to grow.

ROOTS AND CUTTINGS

Theme: plants

Skills: experimenting; observing

Materials: sweet potato

fresh carrot

toothpicks

jar

pie pan

cuttings from ivy, spider plants, begonias, jade plants, or other house plants

clear cups

Directions:

1. Show the children the sweet potato and carrot. Talk about where they grow and what part of the plant they are.

2. Put toothpicks around the middle of the sweet potato. Place it in a jar of water so the pointed end is down in the water.

3. Cut off the top of the carrot (1/2″) and place it in the pie pan with water.

4. Put the plant cuttings in clear cups of water and label.

5. Place the roots and cuttings in a sunny window and add fresh water daily.

6. Keep a journal or draw pictures to record their growth.

Explanation: Some plants grow from roots and cuttings.

COLOR UP

Theme:	plants
Skills:	experimenting; observing
Materials:	clear cups
	food coloring
	celery stalks

Directions:

1. Fill four cups with water. Put a different food coloring in each cup.

2. Place a stalk of celery in each cup and observe what happens for several days. How do the tips of the leaves get colored?

3. Split a stalk of celery halfway up from the bottom. Put one end in the cup with blue food coloring and the other end in the red food coloring. Why does part of the celery turn red and the other part blue?

Challenge: Try this experiment with carnations, daffodils, and other flowers.

Explanation: Water travels up through the stem of the plant to the leaves.

MY BODY

Themes: human body; health

Skills: experimenting; observing

Materials:
latex gloves
wooden dowel or stick
rubber bands
balloon
ziplock bag filled with crackers

Directions:

1. Have the children name various body parts. What covers the outside of their bodies? Compare each other's skin. What will happen if you tear your skin or hurt it? Show the children the gloves and ask how they are like their skin.

2. Next, ask the children to find some bones in their bodies. What do bones do? What happens if you break a bone? Show the stick and ask how their bodies are like the stick.

3. Tell the children there's something else in their bodies that helps them bend and move. See if they can find some muscles in their arms to feel the muscles move. How are the rubber bands like their muscles?

4. Where does the air go when you breathe? Have the children put their hands on their chests and breathe in and out deeply. Can their lungs make their hands move? What happens to the air after they breathe it? How is the balloon like their lungs?

5. Have the children feel their tummies. How is the sandwich bag like this part of their anatomy?

Challenges: Borrow a model of the human body from a high school or college biology lab and let the children explore with it.

Ask the children to draw pictures of what they think they look like inside their bodies.

Explanation: There are many parts of the body that perform different functions.

© 1995 by The Center for Applied Research in Education

HEARTBEATS

Themes: human body; exercise

Skills: experimenting; communicating

Materials: clock with a minute hand

Directions:

1. have the children make their hands into fists. Explain that there's something in their bodies the size of their fists. It works like a motor and pumps blood to all parts of the body.

2. Demonstrate where the heart is and help the children find it on the left sides of their chests. Ask the children to find the veins in their wrists. What's inside their veins? Where else on their bodies do they have veins? Why do they need veins?

3. Does your heart work harder when you're resting or exercising? By checking your pulse you can find out how many times your heart beats.

4. Help the children find their pulses by having them place their index and middle fingers of their right hands on their left wrists. Count the number of times the pulse beats in 15 seconds. (Older children can multiply by 4 to determine how many times it beats per minute.)

5. Next, ask the children to stand up and run in place or do jumping jacks for a minute. Have them sit down again and check their pulses. Compare the pulse rate before and after exercise.

Challenges: Why is it important to exercise? Make a list of all the things children can do to get exercise.

Why is it also important to rest?

Explanation: When you exercise your heart has to pump faster to supply more energy to your body.

BIG SNEEZE

Themes: health; human body

Skills: experimenting; observing

Materials: baby powder or talcum

Directions:

1. Ask the children why it's important to cover their mouths when they sneeze or cough.

2. Demonstrate what happens if they don't cover their sneezes. Sprinkle a little powder on the palm of your hand, then pretend to sneeze on it. What happens to the powder? How are germs like the powder?

3. Practice sneezing and coughing with a tissue as you say this poem:

    When I cough or go kerchoo,
    This is what I always do.
    I cover my mouth with a tissue
    So my germs won't get on you!

Challenge:

Let the children rub some finger paint on the palms of their hands. Have them walk casually around the room for a few minutes talking to other children, playing with toys, and touching different objects. Look around the room at everything that has the paint on it. What happens when you don't wash your hands and you have germs on them? How can you stop germs from spreading?

Explanation: It's important to cover your mouth when you have to cough or sneeze so you don't spread germs.

CLEAN HANDS CLUB

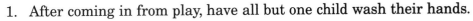

Themes: germs; health

Skills: experimenting; observing

Materials: raw potatoes
2 plates

Directions:

1. After coming in from play, have all but one child wash their hands.

2. Peel the potato, then cut it inhalf. Give one half to the child with dirty hands and the other half to a child with clean hands. Instruct them to rub the potato in their hands, then place it on a plate. Label each potato.

3. Observe the potatoes for several days. (The "dirty hand" potato should have more bacteria growing on it.)

4. What happened to the potato that was in the dirty hands? Why should you wash your hands before eating?

Challenges: Look at the potato with a magnifying glass.

Ask one child to wash his/her hands with water and dry them on a white paper towel. Have another child use soap and water. Compare the difference on the paper towels.

Explanation: Many times there are bacteria on your hands that you cannot see but that can make you sick. You can eliminate germs by washing and drying your hands.

HAPPY TEETH

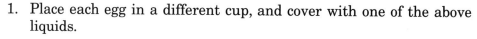

Themes: dental health; human body

Skills: experimenting; communicating

Materials: 4 raw eggs

4 clear cups

tea, coffee, cola, water

Directions:

1. Place each egg in a different cup, and cover with one of the above liquids.

2. Observe the eggs for several days to see what happens

3. Remove the eggs and encourage the children to describe what happened and why.

4. How are teeth like the eggs? What will happen to your teeth if you drink cola, tea, and coffee all the time?

Challenges: Have the children gently brush the eggs with toothpaste and a toothbrush to see what happens

Soak the eggs in other liquids and let the children predict what will happen.

Invite a dentist to talk to the class about dental health and why it is important to brush frequently.

Make a list of foods that are not good for your teeth.

Ask the children to look in the mirror and count the number of teeth in their mouths.

Explanation: The enamel on teeth is stained by certain liquids, but brushing them can remove the stain and help prevent decay.

© 1995 by The Center for Applied Research in Education

III

Discovery Boxes

"Science in a box" is what you will create with these discovery kits. Self-contained discovery boxes encourage children to learn and explore individually or in a small group. They are also a practical way to store materials and organize collections.

Detergent boxes with handles, shoe boxes, or plastic storage containers can all be used for making discovery boxes. Be sure to label boxes with the contents and picture clues. For older children, make task cards with questions and extension activities that they can complete with the items in the box.

You'll also find that discovery boxes are a unique way to encourage parent interaction. Allow children to "check out" the boxes to take home for learning and exploring with their parents. Parents might also be willing to create some of their own discovery boxes with interesting natural objects that they would like to contribute to your science center.

YOUR NOSE KNOWS

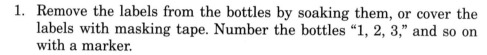

Theme: senses (smell)

Skills: classifying; predicting

Materials: detergent box or grocery sack

empty plastic bottles (mustard, chocolate, syrup, ketchup, lotion, shampoo, salad dressing, and so on)

blindfold

tape and scissors

markers

Directions:

1. Remove the labels from the bottles by soaking them, or cover the labels with masking tape. Number the bottles "1, 2, 3," and so on with a marker.

2. Let the children work in pairs, the first child closes his or her eyes or wears the blindfold. The second partner unscrews the lids of the bottles one at a time for the first child to smell and try to identify. (For older children, have the second child write down the partner's predictions.)

3. Store all the materials in the box or a grocery sack.

Challenges:

Take a "smelly walk" and try to identify different odors in your environment.

Play an association game, such as which one would go with a hot dog? Ice cream? Hair? Hands?

Let children match up labels with plastic bottles.

Explanation: Noses can identify objects by their odors. Noses can warn your brain of danger if there's smoke, or they can tell you if you're having a favorite food for dinner.

© 1995 by The Center for Applied Research in Education

SPICEY MATCH

Theme: senses (smell)

Skill: classifying

Materials: detergent box
index cards
rubber cement
spices (oregano, curry, ginger, cinnamon, garlic, onion, allspice, or nutmeg)
ziplock baggies

Directions:

1. Spread a circle of rubber cement on each end of an index card. Sprinkle the same spice on each circle. Cut the card in half. Store in a ziplock baggie.
2. Make spice cards with each spice and store separately in the baggies.
3. Let the children take out all the crabs, mix them up, then match up like smells.
4. Store all the spice cards in the detergent box.

Challenges: Make word labels on baggies for children to match up spices and words.

Give children food pictures and let them match spices with foods that they go with.

Create a "smell" collage by gluing different spices on a paper plate.

DO YOU HEAR WHAT I HEAR?

Theme: senses (hearing)

Skills: classifying, predicting

Materials: detergent box

                      poster board

                      glue

                      film containers

                      unpopped corn, rice, beans, salt, cotton balls, paper clips

Directions:

1. Cut the poster board into 4″ squares.
2. Glue a small amount of the objects above to different cards.
3. Fill each of the film containers halfway with popcorn, rice, beans, salt, cotton balls, or paper clips. Put on the tops.
4. Have the children shake the cans and match them with the items on the cards. (Number the bottoms of the cans and the cards so they are self-checking.)
5. Place all the materials in the detergent box.

Challenges: Make two of each sound can so children can match up like sounds.

                      Let children make their own sound cans for their friends to try and guess what is inside.

                      Use fewer cans depending on the age and abilities of your children.

                      Let the children make different sounds in the room as their friends close their eyes, then let them guess what made the sound.

Explanation: Different objects make different sounds when you shake them. Your ears can identify objects by the sounds they make.

© 1995 by The Center for Applied Research in Education

TOUCH AND TELL

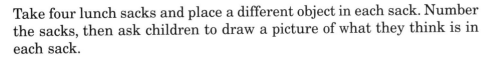

© 1995 by The Center for Applied Research in Education

Theme: senses (touch)

Skills: classifying; inferring

Materials: detergent box

drawstring bag or sack

objects found in nature (bark, pine needles, seeds, pine cones, leaves, egg-shell, flower, rock, bone, feather, animal fur, or shell)

Directions:
1. Place several objects in the drawstring bag or sack.
2. Let the children reach in the bag, try to identity each object, then pull it out to check their predictions.
3. Store the materials in the detergent box.

Challenges:

Take four lunch sacks and place a different object in each sack. Number the sacks, then ask children to draw a picture of what they think is in each sack.

Make pairs of fabric swatches by gluing velvet, terry cloth, corduroy, wool, satin, and flannel to 3″ cardboard squares. Have children close their eyes and match up like fabrics by feeling them.

Fold a piece of paper into fourths. Let children take a crayon and make rubbings of four different textures in the classroom.

Explanation: Nerves in your hands send messages to your brain that help you identify what you feel.

NO BONES ABOUT IT

Themes: bones; animals; human body

Skill: classifying

Materials:
detergent box
Halloween skeleton (lifesized, jointed)
bones from chicken, pork, beef, or fish (soak in bleach water overnight to clean)
pictures of the above animals

Directions:

1. Take apart the skeleton, laminate it, and cut it out. Have the children reassemble it on a butcher paper outline or on the floor.
2. Let the children examine the bones, then match them up to the appropriate animal picture.
3. Place the bones and skeleton in the box.

Challenges:
What would happen if wee didn't have bones? Feel your skull. What does it protect? Feel your ribs. What do they protect?

What happens if you break a bone?

Ask a doctor for some old X-rays that the children can examine.

Why do different animals have different kinds of bones?

Explanation:
People and animals have bones to give them support and protect important organs in their bodies.

© 1995 by The Center for Applied Research in Education

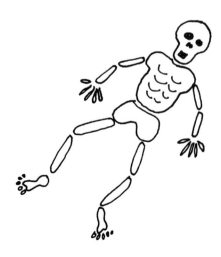

ROCK AND ROLL

Themes: geology; earth

Skill: classifying

Materials: detergent box
magnifying glass
variety of racks
ruler
scale
paper and pencil

Directions:

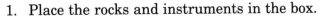

1. Place the rocks and instruments in the box.
2. Let the children sort the rocks and investigate them with the magnifying glass.
3. Have the children weigh and measure the rocks and record their results.
4. Compare rocks and seriate them by size.

Challenges: Take the children on a rock hunt out on the playground.

Ask the children to draw pictures of their rocks with colored pencils.

Starting a rock collection in the science center by inviting friends and relatives in other parts of the world to send rock samples to you.

Brainstorm all the ways that rocks are used.

Invite a geologist to make a presentation to your class.

Create a similar discovery box using seashells.

Explanation: The earth's surface is made up of different kinds of rocks

LEAVES, LEAVES, EVERYWHERE

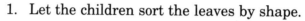

Themes: leaves; trees

Skills: classifying; observing

Materials: detergent box

variety of leaves and needles

magnifying glass

Directions:

1. Let the children sort the leaves by shape.
2. Ask them to sequence the leaves by size.
3. Have them look at the leaves with the magnifying glass.
4. Keep the leaves and magnifying glass in the box.

Challenges: Give children pictures of trees and ask them to match up the leaves to their trees.

Make leaf rubbings

Collect leaves on a nature walk.

In the autumn; collect a variety of colored leaves and ask the children to sort them by color.

Make a discovery box with different kinds of nuts or seeds for the children to explore and sort.

Explanation: Trees grow their own unique leaves that can be identified by their shapes.

© 1995 by The Center for Applied Research in Education

DOWN ON THE FARM

Themes: animals; animal products

Skills: classifying; inferring

Materials: detergent box
toy farm animals (chicken, cow, sheep)
milk carton, egg carton, wool yarn (or other pictures of animal products)
paper and crayons

Directions:
1. Have the children match up the animals with their products.
2. Ask them to draw pictures of other things that come from farm animals
3. Place all the objects in the box.

Challenges: Brainstorm all the products that are made from milk. How are eggs used? What items are made from wool?

Visit a farmer or invite someone from the county extension office to speak to your class.

Explanation: We get food and other products from farm animals.

WHERE DOES IT GROW?

Themes: plants; fruits and vegetables

Skill: classifying

Materials: detergent box
small, plastic fruits and vegetables (available at craft stores)
blue, brown, black, and green felt

Directions:

1. Cut a piece of blue felt 6″ × 12″ and a piece of brown felt 6″ × 12″.
2. Cut a tree trunk from the black felt (approximately 3″ × 2″) and tree leaves from the green felt.
3. Place the blue felt over the brown felt, then put the tree on the blue felt as shown.
4. Ask the children to place the fruits and vegetables according to where they grow. (Below the ground on the brown; above the ground on the blue; or on the tree.)
5. Store the pieces in the detergent box.

Challenges:

Use pictures or cutouts of foods for this sorting game.

Have children sort fruits and vegetables by color or other attributes.

Collect seeds from various fruits and vegetables and let children match them up with the plastic models or real foods.

Explanation: Some foods grow below the ground, some grow above the ground, and some grow on trees and bushes.

WHAT'S IN THE EGG?

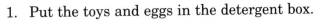

Themes: eggs; animals

Skills: classifying; predicting

Materials: detergent box

large plastic eggs (the ones with a clear half work best)

small toy animals that hatch from eggs (snakes, birds, alligators, fish, frogs, spiders)

toy animals that do not hatch from eggs (dogs, cats, rabbits, monkeys, cows)

Directions:

1. Put the toys and eggs in the detergent box.
2. Let the children place the animals that hatch from eggs in the plastic eggs.
3. How are the other animals born?
4. For self-checking, make a list (words and pictures) of animals that hatch from eggs.

Challenges: Brainstorm all the animals that come from eggs and make a list on a language experience chart.

Hatch chicks in an incubator.

Use small pictures of animals if you don't have toys.

Explanation: Some animals hatch from eggs, but other animals are born live.

FLITTER FLUTTER

Themes: butterflies; life cycle

Skill: communicating

Materials: egg (glue a bean on a paper leaf)

caterpillar (glue pompoms on a popsicle stick or cut the fingers off an old glove and glue them on it to make a puppet caterpillar)

chrysalis (wrap a cotton ball on a stick with thread)

butterfly (color a coffee filter with markers, then gather it in the middle with a spring clothespin)

crayons and paper

Directions:
1. Let the children sequence the life cycle of a butterfly with the objects in the box.
2. Encourage them to tell a story about it.
3. Ask them to draw pictures of the life cycle of a butterfly.
4. Place all the objects in the detergent box.

Challenges: Make a butterfly net from panty hose and a coat hangar. Go on a butterfly hunt.

Collect dead butterflies and moths and put them in clear plastic boxes. Let children look at them with a magnifying glass.

Dramatize being creepy caterpillars, spinning a chrysalis, then becoming butterflies.

Discuss the life cycle of frogs.

Grow a butterfly garden.

Explanation: Caterpillars go through metamorphosis, changing from caterpillars to butterflies.

BIRDS OF A FEATHER

Themes: feathers; birds

Skills: classifying; observing

Materials: detergent box

variety of real bird feathers such as those from a duck, ostrich, pheasant, peacock, blue jay, and so on (you can collect these or purchase them at craft stores)

pictures of birds

magnifying glass

Directions:

1. Fill the box with the feathers and pictures.
2. Examine the feathers with the magnifying glass.
3. Show the children how to "zip" and "unzip" the feathers with your fingers by running them up and down the spine.
4. Ask them to match up feathers with the pictures of the birds.

Challenges:

How do feathers help birds? (Keep them warm, help them fly, protect them from rain.)

Why do birds need different kinds of feathers on their wings, tails, and chests?

Let the children collect feathers on the playground or around their homes. Try and identify the bird they belong to, or make a poster with them.

What do we use feathers for?

Use a feather duster to paint a large mural.

Explanation: Birds can be identified by their feathers. Feathers help birds fly, provide warmth. and protect them.

ANIMAL SKINS

Themes: animals; skin; multicultural

Skills: observing; classifying

Materials: detergent box

animal skin fabrics, fake furs, imitation leather

plastic animals or pictures of animals

Directions:

1. Cut out swatches of the animals fabrics, fake furs, and leather.
2. Ask the children to match the "skins" to the toy animals or pictures.
3. Store all the materials in the detergent box.

Challenges:

Have the children group the skins by type (stripes, spots, fur, leather).

What other types of skin do animals have? What protects turtles, snails, and beetles?

Compare each other's skin. How are you alike? How are you different?

Collect snake skins, turtle shells, and real furs for the children to explore.

Explanation: Animals have different types of coverings and skin.

PAW PAW PRINTS

Themes: animals; tracks

Skills: observing; inferring

Materials:
detergent box

poster board cut in 4″ squares

school glue

toy animals or pictures of animals (bird, rabbit, deer, duck, squirrel, bear, frog, chipmunk)

paper and crayons

Directions:

1. Using the patterns on the following page, draw animal tracks on the poster board. Trace over the lines on the tracks with glue. Dry.
2. Have the children match up the toy animals or pictures of the animals with their tracks.
3. Let the children make rubbings of the animal tracks with crayons and paper.
4. Put all the materials in the detergent box.

Challenges:

Look for animal tracks on a nature walk.

Take off your shoes, dip your feet in paint, and walk across a large sheet of paper. Compare the "tracks" of the children in the room.

In warm weather, take off your shoes and make footprints on wet sand in the sandbox.

How are each animal's feet adapted to their needs?

Explanation: Animals can be identified by their footprints.

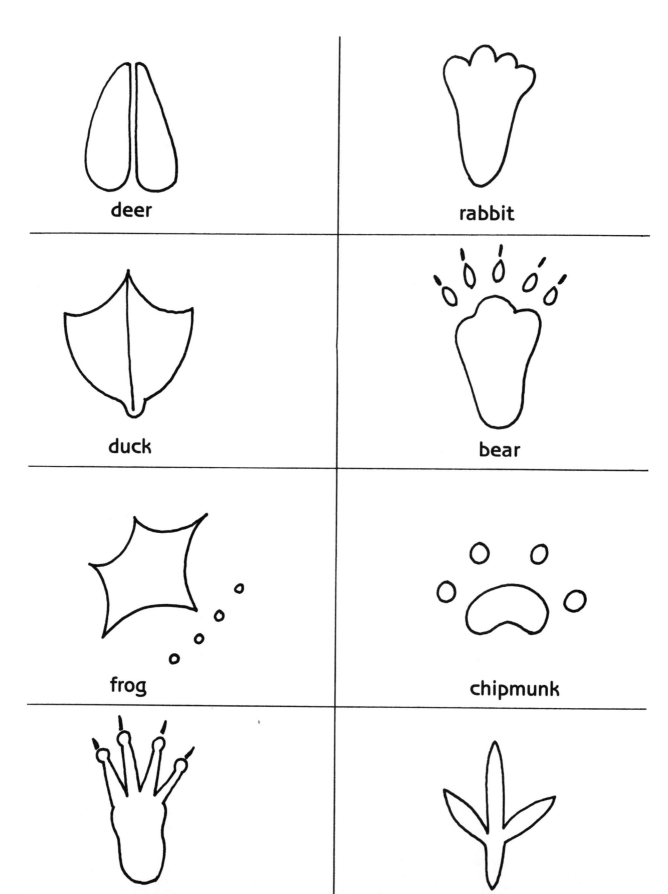

deer

rabbit

duck

bear

frog

chipmunk

squirrel

bird

MIX UP

Theme: colors

Skills: experimenting; observing

Materials: homemade red, yellow, and blue dough (see recipe below.)
ziplock baggies
color chart
crayons and paper
detergent box

Directions:

1. Prepare red, yellow, and blue play dough using the recipe below. Place the dough in separate baggies and store in the detergent box.
2. Make a color chart similar to the one below. Label the words with the colors.
3. Using the color chart, let children take small balls of dough, then mix them together. What new color did they make?
4. Let children make their own color charts with the crayons.

Challenges: Give children eye droppers, food coloring, and an egg carton and let them experiment with making new colors.

For a snack, color two cartons of vanilla yogurt with two of the primary colors. Give each child several spoonfuls of each color in a bowl, then let them stir it up to make a new color. (You might want to use red and yellow on Halloween, or blue and yellow on St. Patrick's Day.)

Explanation: The primary colors (red, yellow, and blue) will make a secondary color (green, purple, orange) when mixed together.

Play Dough Recipe

1 cup salt	2 tbsp. oil
2 cups flour	food coloring
2 cups water	
2 tbsp. cream of tartar	

Mix above ingredients until smooth. Stir in food coloring and cook over medium heat until a ball forms and sticks to the spoon. Knead. Cool. Store in airtight container.

Color Chart

Red + yellow = Orange

Blue + Red = purple

Yellow + blue = green

STICK TO IT!

Theme: magnets

Skills: experimenting; predicting

Materials: detergent box

stationery box with clear plastic top

clear plastic box with small compartments (tackle box or jewelry box)

variety of magnetic and nonmagnetic objects (paper clip, plastic toy, stick, nail, button, balloon, crayon, ribbon, rubber band, pin, and so on)

ring magnet

24″ piece of string.

Directions:

1. Put one item in each compartment of the box. (For young children, tape or glue the box shut.)

2. Tie a magnet to the end of the string, then tape the other end to the box.

3. Let the children experiment with the magnet to see which objects it will attract.

4. Store the materials in the detergent box.

Challenges: Give the children a washable marker and let them predict which objects they think the magnet will attract by marking an "x" on them.

Place small magnetic and nonmagnetic objects in a stationery box with a clear plastic lid. Let the children move a magnet across the lid to see which objects the magnet will attract.

Divide children into partners and give each pair a magnet. Have them go around the room and find objects that the magnet will attract. Older children could make a list of magnetic objects. (Caution children to stay away from computers with magnets!)

Let children experiment with magnets on the playground.

Explanation: Things that are attracted to magnets are called magnetic.

© 1995 by The Center for Applied Research in Education

FIX IT SHOP

Themes: tools; machines

Skills: experimenting; exploring

Materials:

detergent box

screwdriver, pliers, hammer, wrench (use real or plastic tools depending on the age of the children.)

old, broken clocks, radios, or small appliances (ask parents for donations)

screws, nuts, pipes, and connectors

carpenter's apron, safety goggles

Directions:

1. Cut off the appliance cords.

2. Place the tools and appliances in the detergent box.

3. Let the children use the tools to take apart or assemble objects. (Supervise carefully!)

Challenges:

Talk about the tools, how they are used, and the different workers that use them.

Brainstorm all the machines used around your home or school.

Cut out magazine pictures of machines and make a mural with them.

Provide children with woodworking activities.

Add toy tools, a carpenter's apron, safety goggles, and hard hats to the block center.

Explanation: Machines and tools make our work easier.

IV

Nature
Club

Open the door and go out and explore all the wonderful things in your environment. Your playground and community are bursting with plants, animals, and natural objects that will interest and challenge children. Weeds, dirt, and insects you generally pass by can be observed, investigated, classified, and measured. As children explore and learn about their environment, their respect and love for living things will also grow.

NATURALIST'S KIT

Theme: nature

Skills: observing; communicating

Materials:

detergent box with a handle

paper and pencil

magnifying glass

tape measure

magnet

prism

field guide book (birds, trees, rocks, and so on)

compass

plastic glove

ziplock bags and film containers (for collecting specimens)

Directions:

1. Talk about what a naturalist does with the class. What kinds of tools do naturalists use? How are they (the children) like naturalists?

2. Involve the children in making a naturalist's kit they can use to study nature. First, let the children decorate the box with paint or collage materials.

3. Fill the box with the above items and other objects that the children suggest.

4. Take the box on the playground or nature hikes for the children to play with.

Challenges:

Invite a naturalist to come visit your classroom and tell the children about his or her career.

Send directions for making a nature kit home to parents.

Explanation:

Naturalists are people who study nature. They use many tools to do their jobs.

DISCOVERY WALKS

Themes: nature; senses

Skills: observing; communicating

Materials: none

Directions:

1. Change an ordinary outing into a discovery walk by using different senses. One day, tell the children they are going to use their noses to discover new things. Let them smell trees, dirt, leaves, plants, rocks, and other things along the way. What smells good? What smells bad?

2. Another day, take children on a walk and tell them to use their ears and try to remember all the sounds they hear. (You might want to have them sit on the ground and close their eyes for several minutes and focus on the sounds.) When you set back to the classroom, make a list of everything they heard. On another day, take a tape recorder and record different environmental sounds.

3. Use your hands to explore one day. Find objects that are rough, smooth, bumpy, soft, hard, heavy and light. Have children compare the way the bark on different trees feels, or the way different rocks and leaves feel. Play a game where the children close their eyes and try to identify objects by how they feel.

4. Tell the children their eyes will be their cameras and "take pictures" of all the things they will see on a nature walk. Draw pictures of their favorite things when you return to the classroom.

Explanation: Your senses help you take in information and learn new things.

TEXTURE CARDS

Themes: senses (touch); nature

Skills: classifying; communicating

Materials: 3″ × 5″ index cards (or poster board cut this size)
glue
2″ × 3″ samples of the following textures:

burlap	sponge
corrugated cardboard	satin
aluminum foil	sticky tape
sandpaper	scrub brush
felt	cotton
bubble wrap	other textures

Directions:

1. Glue one of the above textures on each card.
2. Take the children outside on the playground or on a nature walk. Give each child or a pair of children a card and ask them to find something in nature that feels like their cards.
3. Encourage the children to describe how their cards feel (rough, smooth, bumpy, sticky, soft) and how the objects in nature feel.

Challenges: Discuss if the objects on the cards are natural or processed. Make a list of things that are natural and processed.

Make a mosaic of different textures.

Do rubbing of different textures in nature.

Explanation: Many processed textures are similar to natural textures found in nature.

© 1995 by The Center for Applied Research in Education

COLOR CARDS

Themes: colors; nature

Skills: observing; classifying

Materials: 3″ × 5″ index cards

                     construction paper in assorted colors

                     scissors

                     glue

Directions: 1. Cut 2″ squares from each color of construction paper and glue them to the index cards

                     2. Give each child a color card and challenge them to find something in nature that matches the color as you walk along on a nature hike.

Challenges: Use color cards as a matching activity in the classroom, asking the children to find toys and other objects that match the colors on their cards.

                     Adapt colors to different seasons and your environment.

                     Give each child a different color of crayon to match up out on the playground.

                     Pass out multicultural crayons and let children match them up with each other's skin color.

                     Sort objects in nature by their color.

                     Collect a variety of leaves of different shades of green and seriate them from dark to light.

Explanation: There are many different colors in nature

TEENY TINY TREASURES

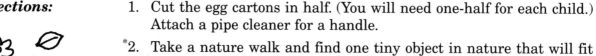

Theme: nature

Skills: classifying; observing

Materials: egg cartons
pipe cleaners

Directions:

1. Cut the egg cartons in half. (You will need one-half for each child.) Attach a pipe cleaner for a handle.
*2. Take a nature walk and find one tiny object in nature that will fit in each section of the egg carton.
3. Encourage the children to share their treasures with their friends and families.

Challenges:

Ask the children to sort the objects in their collections. Which ones are living or nonliving? Are any the same color? Which one is the smallest?

Let the children look at their treasures with a magnifying glass.

Take a field trip to a science museum and make a list of all the different kinds of collections.

Ask the children what they should do with the objects when they don't want them any more. How can they recycle the items, rather than throwing them away?

Explanation: There are many beautiful things in nature that are fun to collect.

© 1995 by The Center for Applied Research in Education

---

*Remind children not to pull leaves or flowers off plants, but to look for objects on the ground.

STREAM CATCHER

Themes: water; nature

Skills: observing; classifying

Materials: coat hanger
old hose
cloth tape

Directions:

1. Bend the coat hanger into a diamond shape.
2. Cut off one leg of the panty hose and pull it over the coat hangar. Tie it at the bottom.
3. Bend the hook on the hanger and tape in place so there's no sharp edge.
*4. Take a walk or field trip to a stream near your school.
5. Let the children use the stream catcher to try and catch fish, plants and other objects in the stream. Try to identify the items.

Challenges:

Put some water from the stream in a jar and take it back to school to examine.

If you go in the spring, you might catch some tadpoles that you can keep as they turn into frogs.

Place ping-pong balls in a stream, then observe the water flow by watching how the balls float. (Children can also toss leaves and flowers in a stream and observe how they flow.)

Explanation: Many living things can be found in streams.

---

*This activity is great fun, but also requires careful adult supervision. Children may also need to wear rubber boots for protection when they do this.

CRITTER KEEPER

Themes: insects; reptiles

Skills: observing; communicating

Materials:
plastic bottle (bleach or 1/2 gallon milk jug)
panty hose
scissors
twist tie
cup
magnifying glass

Directions:
1. Cut 2 or 3 windows in the bottles with scissors.
2. Ask the children to find sticks, leaves, and grass to put in the bottom of the bottle
3. Cut off one leg of the panty hose and stretch it over the bottle.
*4. Show the children how to catch a bug, caterpillar, lizard, or other critter *carefully* with a cup and put it down in the bottle.
5. Put a twisty tie at the top so it doesn't get out, and let the children observe it or look at it with a magnifying glass.
6. After 10–15 minutes, have the children put their critters back where they found them.

Challenges:
What would happen to your critter if you kept it in the bottle and didn't put it back where you found it?

Give children yogurt cartons and have them punch holes in the top. Ask them to find something an insect could live on or something it could eat to put in their containers, then let them catch bugs.

Explanation:
You can catch small animals and observe them to learn more about them, but they need to be set free after a short time.

© 1995 by The Center for Applied Research in Education

---

*Supervise children carefully so they don't try to catch bees and other poisonous insects.

BUG BUFFET

Theme: insects

Skills: experimenting; observing

Materials:
bread crumbs
apple slices
shredded carrot
grass
cheese
cookie
cereal

Directions:

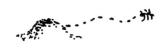

1. Discuss different places you have observed bugs out on the playground. What do bugs like to eat? Make a list of the items that the children suggest.

2. In a quiet corner of the school grounds, create a "buffet" for the bugs. Sprinkle bread crumbs, apple slices, shredded carrots, cheese slices, cookies, cereal, and other foods suggested by the children on the ground.

3. Observe the food and see which insects come to feast. What are their favorite foods?

4. Have the children draw pictures of the insects and their paths.

Challenges: Observe the "bug buffet" for several days and record what happens.

What would insects on the playground eat if you didn't feed them?

Explanation: Bugs are insects that need to eat like all animals. They eat plants or other food that people leave behind.

ANIMAL SAFARI

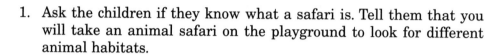

Themes: animals; habitats

Skills: observing; predicting

Materials: paper and pencils

Directions:

1. Ask the children if they know what a safari is. Tell them that you will take an animal safari on the playground to look for different animal habitats.

2. Look for animals on the ground, underground, and in the air.

3. Look for clues as to what an animal may eat, such as a nibbled leaf or cracked nut.

4. Look for where animals might sleep, such as nests, holes in the ground, and so on.

5. Where would the animals get water?

6. Make a list of all the animals you see on your safari. Make a list of animals you do not see, or clues that indicate they might live there.

Challenges:

Hide stuffed animals on the playground, then take an animal safari to find them.

Go on an animal safari in different seasons of the year and compare findings.

Explore different areas in your community for animal habitats, such as parks, woods, or streams.

Explanation: All animals need food, water, and shelter in their habitats to survive.

NIGHT EYES

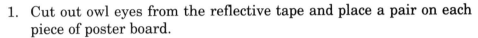

Themes: animals; night

Skills: observing; commmunicating

Materials:
reflective tape
poster board cut in 4″ × 6″ rectangles
scissors
masking tape
flashlight

Directions:
1. Cut out owl eyes from the reflective tape and place a pair on each piece of poster board.

2. Write clues on the cards similar to the ones below:

   - When the moon is bright and you hear not a sound,
     these creatures are busy in their forest town.
     Take the flashlight and shine it bright,
     and you'll find some night eyes on this hike.

   - Whoo-whoo what do I see?
     I see an owl up in a tree.

   - If you're quiet as a mouse,
     You may see me down by my house.

   - Next look for a possum without a sound.
     He's in a tree hanging upside down.

   - A raccoon is the next to spy.
     He wears a mask around his eyes.

   - Although he's blind as a bat at night,
     His radar ears help him with his flight.

   - The hike is over, but keep looking around.
     Are there any other nocturnal animals to be found?

3. Tape the clues to appropriate places outside.

*4. Give the children the flashlight and let and let them find the clues by shining the light on the reflective tape.

Challenges: Hide a treat for the children by the last clue. Play this game inside. Turn off the lights and let children shine the light to look for the clues.This idea is great for overnights or camp-outs.

Explanation: Nocturnal animals come out at night, rather than in the daytime.

---

*This activity works best on a dark day or early in the evening.

LEAF HUNT

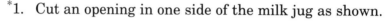

Themes: plants; leaves

Skills: classifying; observing

Materials: plastic milk gallon
scissors
permanent markers

Directions:

*1. Cut an opening in one side of the milk jug as shown.

2. Let the children decorate their milk jugs with markers.

3. Go on the playground or on a nature walk and ask the children to find as many different kinds of leaves as they can put in their jugs. (Remind them to collect only one of each leaf, and to pick up leaves off the ground only.)

4. Count to see how many different leaves they found. How are their leaves alike? How are they different? Are they all the same color and shape?

5. Try to identify the trees that the leaves came from.

Challenges: Put everyone's leaves together and then sort them.

Show the children how to crumble up brown leaves and turn them into soil. (Simply rub the leaves between your two palms to do this.)

Hunt for flowers, nuts, rocks, or seasonal items.

Go to the library and check out a book on leaf identification.

Explanation: Different kinds of plants grow their own unique leaves. You can identify a plant by its leaves.

© 1995 by The Center for Applied Research in Education

---

*An adult will need to do this.

NUTSY

Themes: trees; nuts

Skills: classifying; observing

Materials: sacks, baskets, or pails
forest or woods with deciduous trees
bag of mixed nuts in the shells (purchase at grocery store)

Directions:
1. Go on a nature walk and collect nuts. Try to identify the nuts and match them up with the tree they came from.
2. After collecting the nuts, sort them. (If there are no nuts in your playground, take a bag of mixed nuts and hide them for the children to find.)
3. Crack the nuts open to see what is inside. Which animals need nuts for food? What will happen to the nuts left on the ground?

Challenges: Crack the nuts from the grocery store and eat them for snack. (An adult will need to do this.)

In the fall, prepare a special place in your garden or on the playground and plant some of the nuts you find. Watch to see if they will grow in the spring.

Collect pine cones from the coniferous trees and observe them. Do they have seeds?

Explanation: Some deciduous trees produce nuts that can grow into new trees.

PLANT A TREE

Themes: trees; Arbor Day

Skills: experimenting; communicating

Materials: tree seedlings (available from the Forestry Service or the National Arbor Day Foundation)
shovels
spray bottles

Directions:

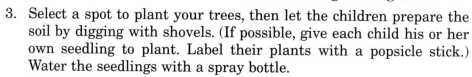

1. Order seedlings from your local Forestry Service or write the National Arbor Day Foundation.
2. Discuss the life cycle of a tree and all the things trees give us.
3. Select a spot to plant your trees, then let the children prepare the soil by digging with shovels. (If possible, give each child his or her own seedling to plant. Label their plants with a popsicle stick.) Water the seedlings with a spray bottle.
4. Encourage the children to draw pictures of their trees, measure them, or keep other records of their trees.

Challenges: This is a great activity for Arbor Day or Earth Week.

Have a fund-raiser so children can earn their own money to purchase the seedlings.

When a child has a birthday, ask parents to plant a tree or bush in the playground to commemorate the special day.

Explanation: Trees are a renewable natural resource that help clean the air, provide shade, protect us, serve as a home for animals, and make the world more beautiful.

Address for the National Arbor Day Foundation:

National Arbor Day Foundation
100 Arbor Avenue
Nebraska City, NE 68410

WONDERFUL WEEDS

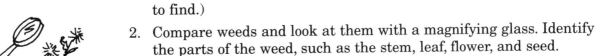

Themes: plants; weeds

Skills: observing; classifying

Materials: magnifying glass

Directions:

1. Go outside and hunt for weeds. (Dandelions are usually the easiest to find.)
2. Compare weeds and look at them with a magnifying glass. Identify the parts of the weed, such as the stem, leaf, flower, and seed.
3. How do weed seeds get planted all over? How does the wind help plant seeds? How do birds and other animals plant seeds?
4. How do weeds help the earth? Why don't some people like weeds?

Challenge: Let one child put on an old sock over his or her shoe as you go on a nature hike. (Make sure to walk through some weedy areas.) When you return to the room, put the sock in a ziplock bag, water it, and hang it in a sunny window. You'll have a sock that grows!

Explanation: Weeds have seeds that are scattered by the wind and other animals.

STICKY BRACELET

Themes: nature; plants

Skills: observing; creating

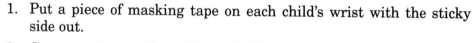

Materials: wide masking tape
natural objects

Directions:

1. Put a piece of masking tape on each child's wrist with the sticky side out.
2. Go on a nature walk and have children collect small flowers, leaves, and seeds to stick to their bracelets.
3. What happens if the objects are too heavy or too big?

Challenges: Make an autumn bracelet in the fall from colored leaves or a spring bracelet of flowers.

Cut a piece of clear contact paper to fit around the wrist. (It can be the same size as the masking tape.) After children have attached leaves and flowers to it, cover the bracelet with another piece of clear contact paper.

Explanation: Beautiful objects in nature can be used in many ways.

CLASS GARDEN

Themes: plants; food

Skills: experimenting; observing

Materials: garden spot
child-sized garden tools
seeds
watering cans or spray bottles

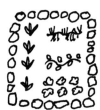

Directions:

1. Select a spot for your garden, then ask a parent to come help you till it. (Use landscape timbers or rocks to outline the area.)

2. Let the children decide which vegetables they would like to grow, then purchase the seeds.

3. Read the directions on the seed packets and make a diagram of the garden to outline where to plant different seeds.

4. Several days before planting, encourage the children to dig in the dirt with their tools and shovels.

5. Let the children make the rows, plant the seeds and water their garden. (Label each row.)

6. Have the children care for their plants by pulling weeds and watering them throughout the summer.

7. Encourage the children to "harvest" their vegetables and prepare them for snack or lunch.

Challenges: Are there any winter vegetables that grow in your area that you could plant in the fall?

Make a scarecrow for your garden. Stuff old hose with leaves and straw for the arms and legs, then dress it in old clothes. Make a head from a grocery stack and stick on a funny hat.

Explanation: You can plant seeds and grow your own food.

SNAIL MASK

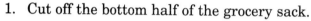

Themes: snails; senses (seeing)

Skills: experimenting; observing

Materials:
paper grocery sack

scissors

wax paper

tape

Directions:

1. Cut off the bottom half of the grocery sack.

2. Cut a 6″ × 8″ rectangle out of one side of the bag as shown.

3. Tape wax paper over the rectangle to make a snail's mask. (Snails can't see well, so looking through the wax paper stimulates their vision.)

4. Discuss the characteristics of snails, such as how they move, what they eat, and how their shells protect them. How do you think snails find food if they can't see well?

5. Go out on the playground and let the children take turns putting on the snail mask and crawling around looking for food.

Challenges:

Let the children make their own snail masks and decorate them with paints and markers.

How are snails and slugs different? How are they alike?

Cut out pictures of foods and nonedible items. Let the children put on the snail mask and see if they can discriminate the foods.

Explanation:

Snails belong to a group of animals called mollusks.

© 1995 by The Center for Applied Research in Education

BLIND AS BATS

Themes: animals; bats

Skill: communicating

Materials: none

Directions:

1. After talking about bats and their characteristics, discuss how bats can fly around even if they can't see. Explain that bats emit a high squeaky sound that bounces off objects. Since objects make different echoes, bats can tell the difference between a tree, cave, or bush.

2. Go outside and let one child be the bat and stand in the middle of a circle. Choose several other children to be "trees," "bushes," "caves," "mountains," or "rivers." Instruct them that when the bat "squeaks," they must respond by saying what they are, such as "tree," "cave," "bush," and so on.

3. The bat closes his or her eyes, turns around three times, and then begins to "squeak" as other classmates call out what they are. The bat follows the sound and tries to find the other children. Keep playing until the bat has found everyone.

4. As children become more adept at this game, scatter them on the playground rather than having them stand in a circle.

Challenges:

Go to the library and check out books on bats.

Invite someone who raises bats to be a guest speaker. How do bats help us?

What kind of similar technique do pilots use to fly their planes when it is dark or cloudy?

Explanation:

Bats make little squeaks that bounce back from objects in their path. Their sharp ears pick up the echo, enabling the bat to fly.

BUG HUNT

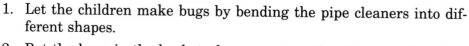

Themes: birds; camouflage

Skill: observing

Materials: pipe cleaners of different colors (red, yellow, green, brown)
basket

Directions:

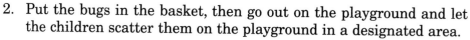

1. Let the children make bugs by bending the pipe cleaners into different shapes.
2. Put the bugs in the basket, then go out on the playground and let the children scatter them on the playground in a designated area.
3. Tell the children that they are baby birds and that you're their mother and you want to teach them how to hunt for bugs. Ask them to go find a red bug and bring it back to you and put it in the basket. Next ask the children to find yellow bugs, then a green bug, finally, a brown bug.
4. Which bugs were easiest to find? Which ones were more difficult to find? Why?

Challenges: Discuss other plants and animals that are camouflaged. Why is it important for them to blend in with their surroundings?.

Color a picture, camouflaging a mystery object for others to find.

Explanation: It is more difficult to find animals that are the color of their surroundings.

CAMOUFLAGE

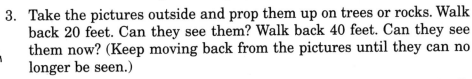

Themes: camouflage; animals

Skills: observing; communicating

Materials:
white paper
crayons and paint
scissors

Directions:

1. Ask the children to draw a picture of an animal they might see in the woods or on the playground.

2. Have them color or paint the pictures and cut them out.

3. Take the pictures outside and prop them up on trees or rocks. Walk back 20 feet. Can they see them? Walk back 40 feet. Can they see them now? (Keep moving back from the pictures until they can no longer be seen.)

4. Turn the pictures over so they are white and prop them up. Walk back 20 feet. Can they see them? Walk back 40 feet. Can they see them better when they are white?

5. How do animals' colors camouflage and protect them?

Challenges:

Think of other animals that are camouflaged. Why are horseshoe rabbits white in the winter and gray in the summer?

Who might wear camouflage clothing for their jobs? Why?

Would you wear the same clothes if you were trying to camouflage yourself in the desert or jungle? Why not? Which color would you wear in the desert? Jungle? North Pole?

Explanation:

Some animals are camouflaged to blend in with their environment. This protects them from other animals.

NESTING

Themes: birds; nests

Skills: observing; creating

Materials: bird nests
magnifying glass
tweezers

Directions:

1. Go on a nature walk and look for abandoned bird nests. (You might want to send a note home to parents asking them to look around their yards with their children for nests.)

2. Observe materials that birds use to build nests. How do they make everything stick together? How do birds build nests without hands?

3. Cut the nest in half and dissect it with tweezers. Look at it with a magnifying glass.

4. Let the children collect twigs, leaves, string, and other materials and try to duplicate a bird's nest. Can they do it as well as the birds? Why not?

Challenges: If you have several nests, compare the different materials used, size, shape, and so on.

Check out a book from the library with illustrations of different birds and nests.

Water a nest and observe it for several weeks to see if it will "grow." (Often seeds will sprout from nests.)

Let children build a nest in a margarine tub with dirt mixed with glue, straw, and twigs. Make clay eggs to go in the nest.

Explanation: Birds build nests in which to lay their eggs. Different kinds of birds build different nests.

NEST IN A BASKET

Themes: birds; nests

Skill: observing

Materials:
berry baskets
mesh potato or fruit bags
straw, grass, pine needles, twigs
string, yarn

Directions:

1. After observing materials birds use to build nests, let children collect similar items from the playground or their homes.

2. Cut up short pieces of string and yarn.

3. Have the children weave the string, yarn, straw, and grass through the berry baskets and mesh vegetable bags.

4. Hang the baskets and weavings from trees on the playground.

*5. Observe the birds to see what items they use. Try to follow the birds to see where they build their nests.

Challenge: Which items do the birds prefer?

Explanation: Birds use many different materials to build nests.

---

*This project will be more successful in the early spring.

© 1995 by The Center for Applied Research in Education

BIRD BREAD

Themes: birds; bird feeders

Skill: observing

Materials:
stale bread
egg white
bird seed
cookie cutters
straw
string or yarn
paint brush

Directions:

1. Cut out shapes from the bread with the cookie cutters.
2. Poke a hole in the shape with a straw, and tie on a piece of string or yarn as a hanger.
3. Brush the egg white on the bread, then sprinkle on bird seed..
4. Dry. Hang outside from a tree.

Challenges:

Use leftover biscuits, bagels, buns, or other breads to make bird bread.

Observe to see which kinds of birds eat the bird bread. Which spot do they prefer to eat from?

String raisins, cranberries, popcorn, and marshmallows to make a chain. Hang from tree and observe which is the birds' favorite food.

Explanation: Birds need to be fed in the winter when there is not much food for them to eat.

© 1995 by The Center for Applied Research in Education

PLAYGROUND FEEDERS

Themes: birds; bird feeders

Skills: observing; creating

Materials:
milk jug or carton
pine cones
bird seed
peanut butter and sand
large pretzels
toilet paper rolls
scissors, string

Directions:

1. Let children design and construct bird feeders using the above materials.

2. Holes can be cut in the milk jugs and cartons, and filled with bird seed. Attach a string for a hanger and a stick or a twig for a perch.

3. Mix the peanut butter with sand. (This will keep the birds from choking on the peanut butter and will aid in their digestion.) Spread the peanut butter mixture on pretzels, toilet paper rolls, or pine cones. Sprinkle with bird seed and attach a piece of string for hanging.

4. Hang the bird feeders on your playground and be bird watchers.

Challenges: Check out a book on birds and try to identify some of the birds you see.

How are birds alike? How are birds different?.

Explanation: There are many different types of bird feeders that you can make.

DIG IT

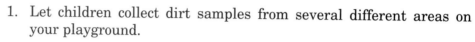

Theme: dirt

Skills: observing; classifying

Materials: shovels or large spoons
plastic containers
magnifying glass, tweezers
newspaper

Directions:

1. Let children collect dirt samples from several different areas on your playground.
2. Spread out the dirt samples on the newspaper and compare them.
3. use the magnifying glass to look for small particles in the dirt. Can you tell a story from the bits and pieces of things you find in the dirt?
4. Use the tweezers to separate the rocks, sticks, leaves, and other objects.

Challenges:

Make dirt by digging a hole and crumbling up leaves, dead flowers, bark, sticks, and other natural objects in it. Cover with dirt and label. Come back in a month and dig up the hole and observe what has happened.

Write grandparents and friends in different parts of the country. Ask them to dig up a little of their soil and send it to you in a plastic bag. Compare soil samples. (Collect soil samples from other countries if possible.)

Make a mud painting by adding a little water to the dirt samples and applying it to paper with a paint brush.

Explanation: Dirt is made from rocks and other decaying materials. The composition of dirt varies in different parts of the world.

ROCK BONDING

Theme: rocks

Skills: observing; communicating

Materials: rocks
basket

Directions:

1. Have the children find a special rock on the playground.
2. Ask them to sit down and get to know theirs. Feel, smell, hold, and name them.
3. Have the children put their rocks in the basket, then sit in a circle.
4. Pass the basket around, having each child identify their special rock. (If they can't find it the first time, pass the basket on and they may be able to identify it from those left.)
5. Ask children to tell the group how they knew which rock was theirs.

Challenges:

Play a similar activity with shells, sticks, leaves, and other natural objects.

Let children wash their rocks and use them for an art project.

Explanation: Rocks have different sizes, shapes, and textures.

SUN AND SHADE

Themes: sun; shadows

Skills: experimenting; predicting

Materials: outdoor thermometer

Directions:

1. Have the children stand in the sun, then stand in the shade. Which is cooler? Warmer? Why?

2. Use the outdoor thermometer to measure the temperature both in the sun and in the shade. Compare.

3. Where would you rather play in the summer when it is hot? Where would you like to play in the winter when it is cold?

Challenges:

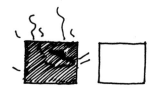

Take out dark colors of construction paper (blue, black, brown, and purple) and light colors (white, pink, and beige). Lay them in the sunshine, then feel them after several minutes. which colors are warmer? Which are cooler? Which colors should you wear on a hot day?

Hang a thermometer in the classroom and outside near a window. Compare the differences or record the temperatures on a graph.

Explanation: It is cooler in the shade because the sun's light and heat are blocked.

© 1995 by The Center for Applied Research in Education

RAIN GAUGE

Themes: weather; rain

Skills: observing; communicating

Materials: plastic jar (cylinder shape)

permanent marker

ruler

Directions:

1. Ask the children how they can tell when it has rained. Does it always rain the same amount? Explain how a rain gauge can be used to measure the amount of rainfall.

2. Demonstrate how to make a rain gauge by marking inch levels on the side of the jar.

3. Have children help you find a good place on the playground for the rain gauge. Why shouldn't it go under a tree?

4. Observe the rain gauge and record the amount of rainfall. Graph the amount that falls each week.

Challenges:

Look at the rain water with a magnifying glass. Is it clean or dirty? Why?.

Why would meteorologists and framers use a rain gauge?

Where does the rain go after it falls to the earth? What happens to puddles when they disappear?

Tell parents about your rain gauge in your newsletter and encourage them to make one at home.

Explanation:

A rain gauge is a tool used by scientists to measure the amount of rainfall.

NORTH, SOUTH, EAST, AND WEST

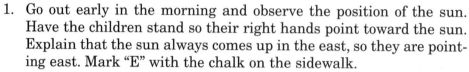

Themes: compass; directions

Skills: observing; predicting

Materials: compass
                   chalk

Directions:

1. Go out early in the morning and observe the position of the sun. Have the children stand so their right hands point toward the sun. Explain that the sun always comes up in the east, so they are pointing east. Mark "E" with the chalk on the sidewalk.

2. The opposite of east is west, and the sun will always set in the west. Have the children extend their left hands and point to the west. Mark "W" on the sidewalk.

3. North will always be in front of you, and south will always be in back of you. Have children point to north and south, then mark "N" and "S" on the sidewalk with chalk.

4. Take the compass and demonstrate how to read directions with it. Does the compass match up with your directions on the sidewalk?

Challenges: Identify directions in your classroom using the compass.

Point out directions on a map or globe.

Take a compass with you on nature walks and other outings and let children identify directions.

Explanation: A compass has a magnet for a needle. North and South poles act as a giant magnet pulling the compass in a N-S position.

© 1995 by The Center for Applied Research in Education

BLOW ME DOWN

Themes: wind; weather

Skills: observing; predicting

Materials:

windy day	sheet of paper
tissue paper	feather
styrofoam	rock
book	leaf
plastic toy	stick
block	seed
sand or dirt	

Directions:

1. Ask the children to help you collect the above items. Which ones do you think the wind can blow away?
2. Take the children outside and observe the objects one at a time to see if the wind can move them by placing them on a picnic table, piece of climbing equipment, or other raised platform.
3. Make a liost of the objects the wind can blow and cannot blow. Compare. How are objects on each list alike?
4. Is there anything on your body that the wind can blow?

Challenges:

Make a wind tester by stapling a piece of crepe paper or ribbon to a straw. Take it outside to determine if the wind is blowing. From which direction is it blowing?

Can you see the wind? How can you tell if it's windy if you can't see the wind?

How does the wind help us? How does the wind harm things?

Talk about tornadoes and practice for a tornado drill.

Explanation: Wind is moving air.

S'NO FUN

Themes: snow; pollution

Skills: observing; predicting

Materials: clear plastic jar
                   snow
                   magnifying glass

Directions:

1. Fill the jar with snow. (Pack it down.)
2. Ask the children what will happen when the snow melts. Will it take up more space or less space? Why? How long will it take to melt?
3. Take the jar inside and record how long it takes the snow to melt. Mark a line on the jar where it melts down.
4. Look at the melted snow with the magnifying glass. Is it clean? Why not?

Challenges: Refreeze the melted snow and note how it expands when frozen. Mark the difference on the jar..

Look at snowflakes on the playground with a magnifying glass by catching them on black paper.

Explanation: Snow has a lot of air between the flakes, so it takes up less space when it melts. However, when the water freezes it expands to take up more space.

INCREDIBLE ICICLES

Themes: water; ice

Skills: experimenting; observing

Materials:
pie pan

plastic containers

yarn

freezing temperatures

Directions:

1. Take a winter walk and collect little twigs, dead leaves, pebbles, and pine needles.
2. Fill the pie pan and plastic containers with water and drop in the natural objects.
3. Tie a piece of yarn into a loop and place half of it in the water.
4. Let the containers sit outside over night, then pop out the icicles in the morning and hang then from a tree branch.

Challenges:

Predict how long the icicles will last. What will cause them to melt?

Freeze colored water in plastic pails and tubs, then set on the playground and observe them as they melt.

Explanation: When the temperature goes below 0 degrees Celsius or 32 degrees F, then water freezes. Water takes the shape of its container as it freezes.

SKY WATCH

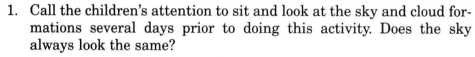
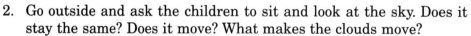

Themes: clouds; weather

Skills: observing; communicating

Materials: blue paper
white chalk
blue sky with cumulus clouds (fluffy, white)

Directions:

1. Call the children's attention to sit and look at the sky and cloud formations several days prior to doing this activity. Does the sky always look the same?

2. Go outside and ask the children to sit and look at the sky. Does it stay the same? Does it move? What makes the clouds move?

3. Give each child a sheet of blue paper and a white piece of chalk and ask them to draw what they see in the sky.

4. Look for animals and other objects in the sky.

Challenges: Read *It Looked Like Spilt Milk* by Robert Shaw.

Take a big sheet of blue butcher paper and hang it on the playground fence. Let the children paint it with white paint to create a mural. Ask them to cut out objects they might see in the sky and glue them to the mural.

Record the cloud formations in the sky for several weeks. Each day choose a different child to sketch what he or she sees.

Explanation: There are different kinds of clouds that represent different types of weather.

SAME AND DIFFERENT

Theme: nature

Skills: observing; classifying

Materials:
2 sticks (from different trees)
2 different kinds of rocks
2 different kinds of leaves
2 different kinds of feathers
snail shell and seashell
2 pine cones, seed pods, nuts, or other items
box or basket

Directions:

1. Encourage the children to help you collect two of the items above and put them in the basket.
2. Ask the children to sit in a circle on the ground and select two objects out of the basket that are alike. Have them describe how they are alike and how they are different. (Do they feel the same? Have the same shape? Are they the same color? Size? Do they smell the same?)
3. Continue passing the basket around the circle as each child selects two like objects and describes their likenesses and differences.

Challenges: Divide older children into pairs and give them 2 similar objects. Have them fold a piece of paper in half and write how the objects are alike on one side and how they are different on the other side.

Do a similar activity with three objects.

Alike	Different
green stems	size shape touch

Explanation: Objects in nature have similarities and differences.

© 1995 by The Center for Applied Research in Education

MYSTERY BAGS

Themes: nature; senses (touch)

Skills: predicting; communicating

Materials: lunch sacks

natural objects (rocks, feathers, leaves, tree bark, bones, fur, antlers, shells, or other interesting items.)

Directions:

1. Place a different object in each bag and fold over the top.
2. Have the children sit on the ground and come up one at a time to select a bag. Ask them to feel what is inside their bag and describe it to the rest of the group. After classmates have had a turn predicting what it is, remove the object from the bag to verify their guesses.

Challenges:

Pass the bags around the circle one at a tine and let each child reach in and feel the object. Tell them to keep what it is a secret until everyone has had a turn.

For older children, number the bags, then let them number their papers and go around and write their answers or draw a picture of what they think each item is.

Explanation: Your sense of touch helps you identify objects by feeling them.

© 1995 by The Center for Applied Research in Education

SCAVENGER HUNT

Theme: nature

Skills: classifying; observing

Materials: sacks
scavenger list

Directions: 1. Divide the children up into groups of 4 or 5.

2. Give a sack and copy of the scavenger list below to each group. (Younger children will need an adult to help them read their lists.)

Scavenger Hunt

Find something smaller than you.

Find something alive.

Find something no longer living.

Find something older than you.

Find something that feels soft.

Find something that is rough.

Find something smaller than your thumb.

Find something that smells good.

Find something green.

Find something yellow.

Find a piece of trash.

Find something that is beautiful.

---

3. Which group can be the first to find all the objects and put them in their sack?

Challenges: Can you find an object for each letter of your name in nature? (For example: S-sand, A-ants, M-moss.)

Dump the objects that everyone finds in a big pile, then try to sort them into groups that are alike.

V

Earth Day, Every Day

Our chidren are growing up in a rapidly changing world, and they will have to face many environmental problems in the future. Our earth is a fragile planet that needs to be loved and protected, rather than abused and neglected. By setting up recycling centers, modeling conservation techniques, and showing concern for environmental problems, we are giving children the skills and attitudes they will need to meet the challenges of dwindling resources, endangered species, and pollution in years to come.

RECYCLE MAN

Themes: recycling; ecology

Skills: communicating; problem solving

Materials:
clean, used aluminum foil
fabric scraps
yarn
wiggly eyes
glue, scissors
paper and pencil

Directions:

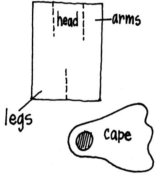

1. Press out the aluminum foil flat and cut as shown.
2. Squeeze and mold the bottom sections to make legs. The top flap will become the head, and the other pieces arms.
3. Cut a cape out of the fabric, and decorate the character with wiggly eyes and yarn hair.
4. Let the children think of an environmental problem (rain forest, trash, water pollution, endangered animals, and so on.) Next ask them to think of a story of how their "Recycle Man" or "Recycle Woman" could solve it. (Younger children could dictate a story while older children could write their own.)

Challenges:
Groups of children can do this project together, making a little skit to perform for the class.

Discuss environmental problems in your community and ask the children how they can help solve them.

Explanation:
There are limited resources on the earth which must be conserved for everyone in the future.

AIR POLLUTION

Themes: pollution, air

Skills: experimenting; observing

Materials: 6 paper plates
petroleum jelly
hole punch
pipe cleaner

Directions:

1. Punch a hole in each plate and attatch a pipe cleaner for a hanger.

2. Spread a small layer of petroleum jelly on each plate.

3. Hang the plates outside in different locations and label. (For example, near a road, by an air vent, under a tree, and so on.) Also, put one under a bus or car exhaust pipe as it starts up.

4. After twenty-four hours, collect the plates and compare the results. What has collected on the plates? Which has more pollution? Why?

Challenges:

What causes air pollution?

What can be done to prevent air pollution?

Hang five plates with vaseline in the same area outside one Monday morning. Take down one plate each afternoon and examine it. What happens the longer a plate remains outside?

Do similar experiments by spreading petroleum jelly on toilet paper cardboard rollers.

Explanation: There are tiny particles of dirt and trash in the air called air pollution.

WATER POLLUTION

Themes: water, pollution

Skills: experimenting; predicting

Materials: 2 large jars of water
                  laundry detergent
                  paper trash
                  styrofoam packing
                  vegetable oil
                  aluminum foil scraps

Directions:

1. Place both jars on the floor. Let the children describe how the water looks, feels, and smells.

2. Let children take turns polluting one of the jars of water by adding a little detergent, torn paper, vegetable oil, and other scraps.

3. Compare the 2 jars now. How do they look? Which one would you like to drink? Which one would you like to swim in?

4. What do you think happens to the fish and plants that live in the water that is polluted?

Challenge: Ask children to collect water samples from streams, ponds, lakes, or other bodies of water in their communities. Compare. Do you see any signs of pollution?

Explanation: Trash, chemicals, oil spills, and other materials have polluted our sources of water.

CLEAN WATER MACHINE

Themes: water: pollution

Skills: experimenting; observing

Materials: clay pot
                   pie pan
                   coffee filter
                   rocks
                   sand
                   jar
                   dirt

Directions:

1. Make a water filter by placing a clay pot in a pie pan. Put a coffe filter in the pot, then a layer of sand and rocks.
2. Mix muddy water by stirring up a little dirt in a jar of water.
3. Slowly pour the muddy water in the clay pot and observe the difference between what was poured in and what collects in the bottom of the pie pan.

Challenges:

Make another jar of dirty water and set it on a brick or thick book. Set another jar on the table below it. Get a 16″ long piece of thick cotton cord or string. Put one end of the cord in the dirty jar and the other end in the empty jar. Observe what happens. How did the water get from one jar to the next?

Visit the water plant in your community to see how it filters water. How does the water get to your house?

Make a list of all the things you can do to conserve water.

Explanation: Water can be filtered to remove particles and make it clean to drink and use in your home.

EROSION

Themes: earth; erosion

Skill: experimenting; predicting

Materials:
sand table
sand or dirt
watering can
plastic bottles

Directions:

1. Have the children pile up the sand to make a "mountain" in the sand table.

2. Let the children take the plastic bottles and squeeze air on the sand. What happens to some of the sand? Why?

3. Pour water over the mountain with the watering can. What happens to the sand? Why?

4. What would happen to a mountain after many, many, years of being exposed to the wind and rain? What other things could wear away a mountain?

Challenges:

Let children try this experiment outside on the playground with a large pile of dirt or sand.

Look for signs of soil erosion around your school or your community. What can be done to prevent soil erosion?

Explanation:

Wind, rain, and other elements in nature wear away at the earth's surface. Grass, Trees, and other plants can keep soil from eroding.

RAIN, RAIN

Theme: rain; pollution

Skills: experimenting; observing

Materials: 2 clear jars
coffee filter
magnifying glass

Directions:

1. Have the children place one jar outside in a place where it can collect rain.

2. After several inches have been collected, bring the jar inside. Observe the rainwater and look at it with a magnifying glass.

3. Place the coffe filter in the second jar, then pour the rainwater through it. Observe the particles on the coffee filter.

4. Talk about how rain water pollutes the earth.

Challenges: Conduct a similar experiment with snow.

How do rain and snow get polluted?

Explanation: Particles from factory smoke, automobiles fumes, and other machine collect in clouds and pollute the rain.

PIECE OF THE PIE

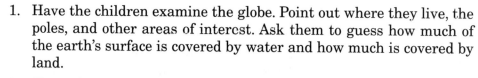

Themes: earth; conservation

Skills: observing; predicting

Materials: large circles (construction paper or poster board)
scissors
globe

Directions:
1. Have the children examine the globe. Point out where they live, the poles, and other areas of interest. Ask them to guess how much of the earth's surface is covered by water and how much is covered by land.
2. Show the children the circle, and tell them that it represents the earth. Cut it into fourths. Put three of the four pieces aside because they represent the area that is coverd by water. Only 1/4 of the earth's surface is land.
3. Cut the fourth in half, because half of the land is not habitable. That means it is too cold, hot, wet, or dry for people to live on.
4. If all people have just a little piece of the earth to live on, what must we do? How can we protect the earth?

Challenge: Tell this story with an apple or pizza.

Explanation: It is important to protect our earth because the amount of useable land is limited.

INSULATORS

Themes: conservation; insulators

Skills: experimenting; predicting

Materials: 2 glass jars
aluminum can
styrofoam cup
dish towel
plastic cup
rubber band
thermometer
pitcher of hot water

Directions:

1. Wrap the dry dish towel around one of the glass jars and rubber-band in place
2. Place the glass jar, aluminum can, styrofoam cup, plastic cup, and glass wrapped in the dish towel on the table
3. Take the pitcher of hot water and fill each container 3/4 full. Ask children to predict which one will keep the water warmest.
4. Place the thermometer in each container at 3 minute intervals and record findings. (Continue until all containers reach room temperature.)
5. Which material is the best insulator?

Challenges:

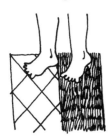

What different kinds of insulators do they use in the walls of homes? In automobiles?

What types of insulators are used to reduce sound?

Take off your shoes and socks. Put one foot on the rug and place your other foot on a tile or wood floor. Which seems warmer? Why?

Put ice cubes in the above containers and compare which one keeps the ice cube from melting.

Explanation: Metal is a conductor of heat, so the can cools more quickly. The dish towel and styrofoam prevent the heat from escaping.

REMINDER CARDS

Themes: conservation; energy

Skills: communicating; creating

Materials: poster board scraps
crayons, markers
tape

Directions:
1. Brainstorm ways to conserve energy and water.
2. Ask the children to design reminder cards to go by light switches, doors, and water faucets.

Challenges: Encourage children to make reminder cards to place around their homes.

Make a list of other things children can do to save energy and other resources.

Explanation: Reducing energy and water use is one of the best conservation principles.

RECYCLE POSTERS

Themes: ecology; recycling

Skills: communicating; creating

Materials:
poster board
markers, crayons
scissors, glue
used foil, newspaper, plastic, and other "trash"

Directions:

1. Have the children pick up trash from the playground or bring materials found in their trash at home.
2. Using these recycled materials, let the children design posers about conserving energy, recycling, litter prevention.
3. Place the posters around the school or community.

Challenges: Decorate a bulletin board with a mural about recyling:

("U" from newspaper)   (Can from foil)   (Logo from paper sacks)   ("2" from plastic bags)

Make a "recycle bulletin board" and encourage children to bring in objects to hang on it with the recycle logo.

Explanation: Many materials that are ofter thrown away can be recycled and used again.

CAN SMASHER

Themes: recycling; ecology

Skills: communicating; observing

Materials:
2 boards (2″ × 4″—2 feet long)

hinge

metal jar lid

screw driver

hammer

nails

Directions:

1. Place one board on top of the other.
2. Screw on the hinge so the boards open and close.
3. Nail the jar lid on the bottom board 6″ from the open end as shown.
4. Place a can in the jar lid. Bring down the top board to crush the can.
5. Save the crushed cans in a box

Challenges:

Ask parents and children to save their cans for you at home.

Save the "pop top" rings from aluminum cans separately as they're much more valuable. How many rings does it take to fill a milk jug?

Make up a story about the life cycle of an aluminum can that gets recycled. Older children can write their own stories, while younger children can dictate a language experience story.

Ask children to bring in used aluminum foil that is clean. Start a ball with it, add to the ball as the year progresses untill you have a giant foil ball.

Explanation: Aluminum cans and foil can be recycled into new products.

BIODEGRADABLE GARDEN

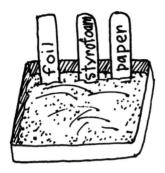

Themes: ecology; gardens

Skills: predicting; experimenting

Materials: tub of dirt or garden

popsicle sticks

aluminum foil, styrofoam, plastic toy, paper, eggshell, leaf

small shovel

Directions:

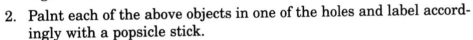

1. Let the children prepare the dirt with garden tools, then let them dig six small holes.
2. Palnt each of the above objects in one of the holes and label accordingly with a popsicle stick.
3. Ask the children to predict which ones they think will decompose and record their guesses
4. After one month, let the children dig up each item and examine the results.

Challenges: Examine the objects with a magnifying glass

Let the children suggest other items that they are interested in, to find out if they decompose or not. Plant these objects and compare results.

Why is it better to use paper cups than styrofoam cups? Why is it better to wrap a sandwich in wax paper than aluminum foil?

Explanation: Some things decompose rapidly, but other things do not and are more harmful to the environment.

OUR DUMP

Themes: recycling; decomposition

Skills: experimenting; observing

Materials:

2 landscape timbers (4′ sections), bricks, or rocks
garbage (fruits and vegetables—no meats)
garden tools

Directions:

1. Prepare a place for your compost on the playground. (A shady spot in an out-of-the way place will work best.)
2. Outline the area to be used with landscape timber, bricks, or rocks.
3. Let the children dig in the dirt for several days to loosen the soil.
4. Find grass, leaves, straw, and other plant clippings to put in the compost. Add vegetable peelings, egg shells, coffee grounds, and other bits of garbage and mix with the dirt.
5. Keep moist and stir every few days. Continue adding more garbage and dead plants to the compost.
6. Abserve the humus that develops in a few months.

Challenges:

Use the humus in the class garden to enrich the soil.

Look at the leaves that have piled up under a tree. What happens to them?

Explanation:

As plants and animals decompose, they turn into humus and become part of the earth.

SAVE A TREE

Themes:	recycling; trees
Skill:	communicating
Materials:	cardboard box newspaper glue paper scraps scissors

Directions:

1. Let the children cover the cardboard box with newspaper and decorate it with paper scraps. Label the box "Save a Tree."
2. Tell the children that whenever they have paper to throw away, they should place it in the box instead of the trash can.
3. How do you "save a tree" when you recycle paper?
4. Take the paper to a recycling center.

Challenges:

Brainstorm other ways to reduce the amount of paper we use by recycling newspapers, reusing grocery sacks, drawing on both sides of paper and so forth.

Ask parents to donate scrap paper from their workplace.

Save junk mail for children to use in the writing center

Use magazines and catalogs for art projects.

Explanation: Paper comes from trees, so when you reuse paper you can save trees.

HOMEMADE PAPER

Themes: recycling; ecology

Skills: experimenting; observing

Materials:
newspaper
blender
screen

Directions:

1. Tear the newspaper into tiny pieces and soak in warm water for 15 minutes.
2. Put the newspaper pulp in the blender and blend for 10–15 seconds.
3. Squeeze out the excess liquid, then pat flat on the screen. (Prop the screen on rocks or bricks.)
4. Dry in the sun for several days.
5. Paint or decorate the homemade paper, foil paper, and other scraps.

Challenges:

Experiment by using funny papers, wrapping paper, foil paper, and other paper scaps.

Add food coloring or glitter to the paper pulp before drying

Make a collage for your classroom or cafeteria with the homemade paper.

Ask the children to look around their homes for products made from recycled paper.

Explanation: Many paper products can be made from recycled paper.

ENDANGERED ANIMALS

Theme: endangered animals

Skills: researching; communicating

Materials: 100 dried beans
books and magazines of endangered animals
lunch sacks
construction paper
scissors, glue
markers and crayons

Directions:

1. Hide the dried beans around the room whole the children are outside. When they come in ask them to hunt for the beans. Count and see how many are found. (They probably won't find all of them.)

2. Challenge them to look for more beans, then count to see how many are found the second time.

3. Ask the children to hunt for beans a third time, and count results. Talk about how each time they looked for beans they were harder to find and there were fewer of them. The same is true with some of the animals on the earth. There are fewer and they are more difficult to find, so they are called *endangered* animals.

4. Make a list of endangered animals. Why are they in danger?

5. Go to the library and find more information on endangered animals.

6. Let the children make puppets of their favorite endangered animals with the lunch sacks.

7. Put on a puppet show. Ask the children why their animals are endangered and what people can do to save them.

Challenge: Write politicians letters about enacting legislation that will save wildlife.

Explanation: Endangered animals are those that have been either hurt or killed in large numbers and are close to extinction.

WEB OF LIFE

Theme: interdependence

Skill: communicating

Materials: pictures of the sun, rain, air, insects, frogs, soil, trees, flowers, rabbits, mice, seeds, and so forth (one for each child)
ball of yarn
tape

Directions:

1. Let children choose their pictures and tape them on.
2. Have the children sit in a circle. Give the ball of yarn to one child who begins the story by saying, "I am" (names picture), and "I need" (names another picture). The first child wraps the yarn loosely around his or her hand, then rolls the yarn to the second child who says, "I am" (names picture), and "I need" (names another picture).
3. The game continues with each child passing the yarn on until they have created a web inside the circle.
4. How do they help each other? Can anything exist alone?

Challenge: Let the children draw their own pictures for this activity.

Explanation: All things in nature are interrelated and depend on each other.

LOVE A TREE

Themes: trees; Arbor Day

Skills: observing; communicating

Directions:

1. Tell the children that your class is going to adopt one special tree on the playground.
2. Take the children outside and let them select their favorite tree. (If the children can't agree, then let them vote on their favorite tree.)
3. Ask the children to name their tree. Get to know the tree by smelling it, listening to it, feeling it, and hugging it.
4. Tell stories or sing songs under the tree.
5. Take pictures of the tree in different seasons, or let the children sketch the tree at different times of the year. When it's hot, let them wash the tree with sponges and water; when it's dry, water it. You might even want to plant flowers under your tree in the summer.

Challenges: Count the trees on the playground. Measure them, do bark rubbings, and compare their leaves.

Write stories and poems about trees.

Discuss ways to conserve trees.

Explanations: Trees need to be loved and cared for like all things in nature.

SIT AND WATCH

Theme: nature; habitats

Skills: observing; communicating

Materials: beautiful day
hula hoops or 8′ piece of string tied in a loop
paper and crayons

Directions:

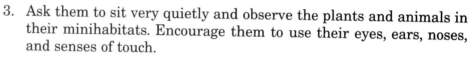

1. Take the children outside on a beautiful day.
2. Have them put the hula hoops or string loops on the ground and sit in them.
3. Ask them to sit very quietly and observe the plants and animals in their minihabitats. Encourage them to use their eyes, ears, noses, and senses of touch.
4. Let the children draw pictures of their habitats outside, or return to the room and make a list of all the plants and animals that they observed.

Challenges: Go on a nature walk and look for animal habitats above the ground, on the ground, and underground.

Conduct a "sit and watch" during different seasons and compare data.

Have the children pretend they are a rock or a tree as they sit outside. How do they feel? What do they hear? What can they see?

Explanation: Animals need food, water, and shelter in their habitats in order to live.

PICTURE PERFECT

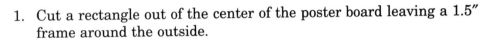

Themes: nature; ecology

Skills: observing; communicating

Materials: poster board cut in half

scissors

Directions:

1. Cut a rectangle out of the center of the poster board leaving a 1.5″ frame around the outside.

2. Take the cardboard frame to a natural area and lay it on the ground. Ask the children to look at the nature picture in the frame and to describe it to you.

3. Tell the children to "mess up" what is in the frame. After they've destroyed it, ask them to make it look as it did before.

4. Can they return it to the original picture? What happens when human beings "mess up" the earth? Can we repair it?

Challenge: Look around your community for areas that have been destroyed by people. Take a field trip to a landfill or other area that has been recycled.

Explanation: Once the earth has been destroyed, it is difficult to return it to its original beauty.

MYSTERY TRAIL

Themes: nature; pollution

Skills: observing; communicating

Materials: paper bag

aluminum can, candy wrapper, styrofoam cup, plastic bottle, old toy, newspaper, plastic bag, and other bits of trash

Directions:
1. Before taking the children on a nature walk, hide the above pieces of trash along the route you will follow.
2. Explain to the children that you will take them for a walk along a mystery trail that's littered with trash. Tell them that they will need to be detectives and find the objects that don't belong in nature.
3. As you go along the trail, let the children collect the trash and put it in a bag.

Challenge: What happens when people don't throw their trash away? How does it hurt nature?

Explanation: People should throw their trash in garbage cans so it doesn't litter the earth.

© 1995 by The Center for Applied Research in Education

EARTH PATROL

Themes: recycling; ecology

Skills: observing; communicating

Materials: empty food boxes
thick yarn or string
hole punch
scissors

Directions:

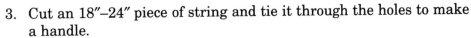

1. Cut off one end of the box.
2. Punch a hole near the top on each side of the box.
3. Cut an 18″–24″ piece of string and tie it through the holes to make a handle.
4. Put the trash pack on your shoulder, go outside and pick up litter,

Challenge: Teach children this rap to say as they pick up trash:

> *Here I go*
> *I'm on the Earth Patrol.*
> *I'm going to work all day*
> *To put the trash away.*
> *The planet earth, you know,*
> *We love so.*
> *I'm going to clean it up*
> *Wherever I go.*

What can we do to keep from having so much trash?

Explanation: When we all do our part and clean up after ourselves, we will have a clean earth.

EARTH QUILT

Themes: nature; Earth Week

Skills: communicating; creating

Materials:
paper
water colors, paints, crayons or markers
hole punch
yarn

Directions:

1. Encourage the children to talk about all the things they love on our earth. (Include plants, animals, and different land forms.)
2. Let them draw or paint a picture about what they like best.
3. Punch a hole in the corners of the pictures, then tie them together with yarn. (You can also tape them together with cloth tape.)
4. How can we protect the things we love in our planet earth?

Challenges:

Use fabric crayons on cloth squares to make a more permanent quilt.

Cut butcher paper into 3″ × 36″ strips. Have each child decorate a strip with a nature scene, plants, or animals. Weave the strips together to make a quilt.

Explanation: With so many things to love, we need to take care of the earth.

RECYCLE FAIR

Themes: recycling; Earth Day

Skills: experimenting; creating

Materials: empty food containers, boxes, bags, newspaper, cardboard rollers, magazines, plastic containers, or other "trashables"

glue

scissors

tape

wire

string

Directions:

1. Ask the children to collect the above items from their homes for a week.
2. Have them bring their junk to school and make a "sculpture" or "invention" to display in the fair. (Children can work independently or in small groups on this project.)
3. Ask children to name their creations and write or tell a story about them.
4. Invite parents or other classes to visit the recycle fair.

Challenges: Choose some recipes from the "Edible Science" chapter to serve at the recycle fair.

Display creations in the library or at a shopping mall.

Set up a recycling center in your classroom or school and encourage your families to participate.

Explanation: It's important to make people more aware of the trash they throw away and how it can be used in new ways.

VI

Artful Expressions

Art and science are a perfect combination, incorporating sensory exploration, experimentation, observation, and creativity. Young children should engage in "process" art that enhances their independence and imagination, rather than "product" art that has a defined outcome. The activities in this chapter will give children the tools to explore, the opportunity to make choices, and the freedom to make something that is uniquely theirs.

NATURE WINDOWS

Theme: nature

Skills: observing; creating

Materials: clear contact paper
natural objects
paper plates

Directions:
1. Let the children collect a few flowers, leaves, feathers, and other small objects on a nature walk.
2. Cut two pieces of contact paper the same size. (12″ squares work well.)
3. Peel the back off one piece and arrange the natural items on it.
4. Peel the back off the other piece and lay it on top, sticky sides together.
5. Hang your "nature window" in a window.

Challenges:

Make a frame for the picture from construction paper.

Make a small nature window, then glue craft sticks around it to make a sun catcher.

Have children arrange natural objects on a paper plate, then cover with clear contact.

SUN PHOTOGRAPHY

Themes: sun; fading

Skills: experimenting; predicting

Materials: blue or purple construction paper

leaves, flowers, feathers, and other objects

rocks

sunny day (no wind)

Directions:

1. Go on a nature walk and ask the children to collect leaves, flowers, and other objects they like.
2. Have the children arrange the objects on the construction paper and place it where it will receive direct sunlight all day. Put rocks on the objects to hold them in place.
3. What will happen to the paper it it's left in the sun all day? What will happen to the areas of the paper covered with leaves and flowers?
4. Have the children collect their papers at the end of the day and observe how the sun has faded the paper.

Challenges: Experiment with different colors of construction paper. Which ones fade more? Less?

Let the children hang out other items and predict which ones will fade. You might try tissue paper, fabric, toys, newspaper, magazines, and so forth.

In the winter, you can do this project by placing the paper in a sunny window for several days.

Order sun-sensitive paper from a science supply store listed in the back of this book.

CHUBBY CHALK

Theme: chalk

Skill: experimenting

Materials:
small paper cups
plaster of Paris
popsicle sticks
tempera paint

Directions:

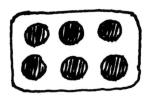

1. Put 1/2 cup of plaster of Paris in a cup.
2. Add a heaping spoonful of tempera paint and stir with a popsicle stick.
3. Add a little water at a time as you stir until it is the consistency of thick gravy. (If you pour in too much water, just add more plaster of Paris.)
4. Let it harden for several hours, peel away the cup, then draw with the "chubby chalk" on the sidewalk.

Challenges:

Experiment with making different colors.

Tear the paper off old crayons. Break up the crayons and put them in a muffin pan. Bake the crayons in the oven on 350° for 5–10 minutes until they melt. Cool. Pop out and color with your chunky crayons.

ROCK 'N' ART

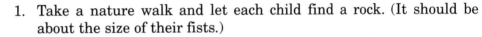

Theme: rocks

Skills: communicating; creating

Materials:
rocks
wiggly eyes
paints
markers
yarn
scissors
glue

Directions:

Rockann

1. Take a nature walk and let each child find a rock. (It should be about the size of their fists.)
2. Let them scrub their rocks at the water table with soap and a brush.
3. Give them the eyes, paints, yarn and other scraps to decorate their rock's.
4. Have the children name their pet rocks and dictate or tell a story about them. (Older children could write their own stories about their rocks.)

Challenges:

Let children make houses for their pet rocks from berry baskets, shoe boxes, or empty food containers.

Pet rocks make charming gifts for parents.

Children can put their pet rocks together to make a "rock band" or a "rock garden" for the classroom.

Give the children different sizes of rocks to glue together to make rock sculptures.

SAND JARS

Themes: sand; colors

Skills: observing; creating

Materials:
sand or salt
colored chalk
plastic bowls
spoons
craft sticks
baby food jars or other small jars

Directions:

1. Pour a cup of sand in each bowl.
2. Let the children take turns stirring the sand with a piece of chalk. (The more you stir, the darker the sand will become.)
3. Make several different colors of sand.
4. Have the children pour or spoon different layers of sand into their jars.
5. Make waves in the sides by inserting the popsicle stick.
6. Seal tightly. (Remind the children to carry their jars carefully or all the colors will get mixed up.)

Challenges:

Dye the sand with tempera or food coloring.

Draw a picture with school glue on a paper plate. Sprinkle with the colored sand, then shake off the excess.

FOSSILS

Themes: fossils; dinosaurs

Skills: experimenting; observing

Materials:
1 cup salt
1 cup flour
1 tsp. alum (available at any pharmacy)
3/4 cup water
bones, leaves, toy dinosaurs, shells

Directions:

1. Mix the dry ingredients together.
2. Slowly add the water until a dough is formed and the mixture sticks together.
3. Roll the dough into balls, then flatten into a pancake.
4. Press the leaves, shells, bones, toy dinosaurs, or other objects in the dough to make an impression.
5. Dry. (Paint if you desire.)
6. Ask the children which objects made the different impressions.

Challenges:

Make fossils with plaster of Paris. (Rub petroleum jelly on the objects before making an impression with them in the plaster of Paris.)

How about fossil cookies? Take "slice and bake" cookie dough and cut off a piece for each child. Let them make thumb prints or use other objects to make impressions in the dough. Cook according to directions.

Make mud dough from dirt, water, straw, and glue. Let children make a pancake around an object, then dry it in the sun for several days. Break it open to reveal a fossil.

NATURE'S FRAMEWORK

Theme: nature

Skills: observing; creating

Materials:
poster board
school glue
twigs, small sticks, small seeds, pebbles, or dried flowers
scissors

Directions:
1. Cut a frame from the poster board. (Any size or shape will work.)
2. Glue the natural objects to the outside of the frame.
3. Tape a photograph or drawing in the frame.

Challenges:

Put nature art (printing, painting, or rubbings) in the frames for gifts.

Go to a shop where they frame pictures and ask them to save matting scraps for you.

Glue four popsicle sticks together to make a frame, then decorate with natural objects.

NEWSPAPER ART

Theme: recycling

Skills: experimenting; creating

Materials: newspapers
                      paint
                      brushes
                      cars
                      junk
                      sponges
                      cookie cutters

Directions:

1. Cut the newspaper in half along the centerfold

2. Let the children experiment with the following painting activities:

    brushes: paint with brushes on the newspaper

    cars: take small cars, dip the wheels in paint, and drive them across the paper

    junk: use spools and toothbrushes, berry baskets, and other "junk" to print designs on the paper

    sponges: cut old sponges into different shapes, dip in paint, and print on the newspaper

    cookie cutters: dip cookie cutters in the paint and print on the paper

Challenges: What other art projects can you do on newspaper (collages, cutting activities, and so on?)

NATURE'S PAINT BRUSHES

Theme: nature

Skills: experimenting; creating

Materials:
feathers
pine needles
twigs
dry straw
leaves
pipe cleaners
pie pans
paint
paper (large sheets or a roll)

Directions:
1. Have the children collect various natural items on the playground.
2. Bundle up the different objects and bind them together with pipe cleaners to make brushes.
3. Pour the paint in the pie pans, then let the children dip the natural brushes in the paint and apply to the paper.

Challenge: Hang butcher paper with clothespins on the playground fence and let the children paint a large mural with the natural items.

© 1995 by The Center for Applied Research in Education

SMELLY PAINTS

Theme: senses (smell)

Skills: experimenting; creating

Materials: tempera paint

cooking extracts and flavors (lemon, strawberry, mint, vanilla, and so on)

brushes

paper

Directions:

1. Add lemon extract to the yellow paint, strawberry to red, mint to green, vanilla to white, and others scents to paints.

2. Give the children brushes and let them paint individual pictures or work together on a class mural.

3. How do the paints smell when they dry?

Challenges:

Add scents to finger paints, play dough, water table, and other sensory materials.

To create different textures, add sand, coffee grounds, glitter, and so forth to tempera or finger paints.

Add a small amount of water to household spices to make paints. Try paprika, cocoa, curry, mustard, and other spices.

RAIN PAINTING

Themes: weather; rain

Skills: observing; creating

Materials: dry tempera
film containers
paper
rainy day

Directions:

1. Poke a hole in the lids of the film containers with sharp scissors or a hammer and nail.
2. Fill each container with a different color of dry tempera.
3. Let the children sprinkle the dry tempera on the paper.
4. Have the children hold their pictures out in the rain as they stand under an awning or covered area.
5. Dry.
6. Ask the children to describe how the rain painted a picture for them, and ask them to name their pictures.

Challenges: Use a spray bottle of water to squirt the paper if it's not raining.

Try this art technique on dark paper for a dramatic effect.

COLOR BLEND

Theme: colors

Skills: experimenting, creating

Materials: paper (large rolls of butcher paper work well)

tempera paints

brushes

squirt bottle or mister

Directions:
1. Let the children paint designs on the paper. Dry.
2. Spray paintings with water, observing the colors as they run and blend.
3. Dry.
4. Cut into shapes or designs.

Challenges:

Cut out giant animals, insects, flowers, trees, planets, and so forth from the painted paper. (Cut two of each shape.) Staple the edges together 3/4 of the way around, then stuff with newspaper strips. Staple remaining section together and hang from the ceiling or wall.

Paint with tempera on a paper towel, then spray with water to blend colors.

SHADES AND PASTELS

Theme: colors

Skills: experimenting; creating

Materials: tempera paint (red, yellow, blue, black, white)
9 plastic cups
paint brushes
water
paper

Directions:

1. Using 3 cups, mix the primary colors. Pour a little of each color into three cups.
2. Add white paint to one cup of each color. What happens to the color? (Adding white makes pastels.)
3. Add black paint to one cup of each color. What happens? (Adding black makes shades.)
4. Paint a picture with the shades and pastels.

Challenges:

Give children paint chips to sequence from dark to light.
Add food coloring to sweetened condensed milk to make glossy pastels.

© 1995 by The Center for Applied Research in Education

MUD PAINTING

Theme: dirt

Skills: experimenting; creating

Materials: plastic containers
shovels or spoons
large paper
paint brushes

Directions:

1. Collect soil samples from several different areas on the playground.
2. Compare the samples and look at the dirt with a magnifying glass.
3. Add water to the different containers of dirt to make thick paints.
4. Paint the mud on the paper with your fingers or a paint brush.

Challenges: Add glue to the dirt to make a paint that sticks better to the page.
Use mural paper and have children work on a mud painting together.

OIL PAINTING

Theme: water

Skills: experimenting; creating

Materials:
cooking oil

cups

spoons

paper

dry tempera (2 or 3 colors)

tub of water

Directions:

1. Pour 1/4 cup of oil in each cup and stir in a spoonful of paint.
2. Fill the tub with water. Dribble a spoonful of each color of paint on the surface.
3. Take the paper, dip it in the tub, then slide it up, catching the paint. (You can also lay the paper on the surface of the water and lift off a design.)

Challenges: Why doesn't the oil mix with the water?

Try this technique with paper plates and different types of paper.

GLUE GLOB

Theme: colors

Skills: experimenting; creating

Materials: school glue
food coloring
heavy paper

Directions:

1. Put a large glob of glue (1–2 tbsp.) in the middle of the paper.
2. Add a drop of blue, yellow, and red food coloring to different corners of the glue. (Do not use green.)
3. Roll the paper around to create colors and design.

Challenges: Try making glue globs on paper plates.

Place a large sheet of butcher paper on the table where you are doing this project to catch the excess glue. Use the spattered paper for the background of a bulletin board.

SPATTER PAINTINGS

Theme: nature

Skills: classifying; creating

Materials: large sheets of paper

natural objects (leaves, flowers, sticks, rocks)

spray bottle

diluted tempera paint

Directions:

1. Arrange the natural objects on the paper. (Do this outside on the playground or in a big box in the classroom.)
2. Pour the diluted paint in the bottle and spray on the paper.
3. Dry.
4. Remove the objects.

Challenges:

Ask the children to identify the objects that made the different shapes on the paper.

Make a matching game in a similar way. Place scissors, crayons, blocks, and other classroom objects on a piece of poster board. Spray with spray paint, dry, then ask children to match up objects with their outlines.

Fill a spray bottle half full with water. Add 10–15 drops of food coloring, then go outside and spray it on big sheets of butcher paper. Use primary colors, then observe secondary colors as they blend together.

MYSTERY PICTURES

Theme: night

Skills: communicating; creating

Materials:
white crayons or candles

paper

blue or black paint, diluted

brushes

Directions:
1. Ask the children to draw a picture of the sky at night with white crayons or candles on a sheet of paper.

2. Let them paint over the paper with blue or black paint that has been watered down.

3. Have children give titles to their pictures or tell stories about them. How are day and night different?

Challenges:
Why doesn't the paint stick where the crayon is?

Write a secret message with a white crayon and give it to a friend. Paint over it to reveal what it says.

You can also do mystery writing with lemon juice. Print a message using lemon juice and a cotton swab. Let it sit in the hot sun, then observe it.

Make an old-fashioned parchment by wadding up a piece of white paper and soaking it in a bowl of tea or coffee. Remove and hang to dry.

FACE PAINT

Theme: colors

Skill: experimenting

Materials: cornstarch
cold cream
red, yellow, and blue food coloring
small cups and spoons
cotton swabs

Directions:

1. Mix 1 tsp. cornstarch and 1/2 tsp. water in a cup.
2. Stir in 1/2 tsp. of cold cream.
3. Add a few drops of food coloring.
4. Apply the face paint with a cotton swab or finger.

Challenge: How can you make purple, orange, and green face paint?

NATURE PRINTS

Theme: nature

Skills: classifying; creating

Materials: leaves, feathers, flowers, seeds, pine cones, rocks, and other natural objects

paper

styrofoam tray

paper towel

thick paint

Directions:
1. Take the children outside and let them collect the objects they will use to print with.
2. Fold the paper towel to fit in the styrofoam tray.
3. Pour a small amount of paint in the tray.
4. Dip one side of the natural object in the paint, then press it on the paper to make an impression.

Challenges: Use several different colors of paint or different colors of paper.

Try to identify the objects by their prints.

When studying about dinosaurs, use meat bones that have been cleaned to make prints.

Let children dip plastic farm and zoo animals in the paint, then "walk" them across their paper to make tracks.

SEEDY VEGGIE PRINTS

Themes: plants; seeds

Skills: classifying; creating

Materials: firm fruits and vegetables (apples, citrus fruits, onion, okra, peppers, cucumbers)

knife

paper towels

styrofoam trays

thick paint

paper

glue

Directions:
1. Cut the fruits and vegetables in half. Remove the seeds and save.
2. Place the fruit halves on paper towels to drain off excess liquid.
3. Line the bottoms of the styrofoam trays with paper towels, then pour in a small amount of paint.
4. Dip the fruit and vegetables in the paint, then press them on the paper to make prints.
5. When the prints have dried, match seeds to the appropriate prints and glue in place.

Challenges:

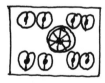

Cut potatoes in half, then carve out designs and use them to print.

Make wrapping paper by printing with fruits and vegetables on tissue paper.

© 1995 by The Center for Applied Research in Education

POUND OUT COLORS

Theme: leaves

Skills: observing; creating

Materials:
white fabric (old sheets work well)
autumn leaves of various colors
wooden board
newspaper
hammer or block

Directions:

1. Cut the fabric into 8″ squares.
2. Let the children hunt for several colored leaves.
3. Lay the fabric on the board, then arrange the leaves on the fabric. Cover with a sheet of white paper.
4. Place several sheets of newspaper on top, and then pound the leaves with the hammer or block.
5. Lift the newspaper, remove the leaves, and observe the colors.

Challenges:

Try to pound the color out of flowers and other parts of plants.

What happens to the color of leaves after they lie on the ground for a few days?

Glue a leaf to a sheet of paper, then create an animal or person out of it with crayons or markers.

Rub old flowers across a sheet of white paper and watch the colors smear.

195

WAX PAPER PRESS

Themes: flowers; leaves

Skills: observing; creating

Materials: flat, natural objects such as leaves and small flowers
wax paper
iron

Directions:

1. Tear off two sheets of wax paper that are the same size.
2. Arrange the leaves and flowers on one sheet, then place the second sheet on top.
3. Iron on medium heat until the wax paper melts together. (An adult will need to do this.)

Challenges:

This is a good project with spring flowers or autumn leaves.

Iron crayon shavings (made by grating old crayons or using a crayon sharpener) between the two sheets of wax paper.

Use wax paper pictures as placemats for snacks.

Collect leaves from different types of trees. Iron each leaf in wax paper separately and label. Put the pages together to make a book.

NATURE'S MOBILE

Theme: nature

Skills: observing; creating

Materials:
stick
feathers
shells with holes
twigs
seeds and nuts
flowers
yarn or dental floss
scissors

Directions:
1. Ask the children to find a stick that is as long as their leg, from their foot to their knee. That will be the base for the mobile.
2. Tie a piece of yarn to the stick so it can be hung up.
3. Let the children collect feathers, leaves, flowers, seeds, and other natural objects they would like to hang from their mobiles.
4. Have them tie the objects to their sticks with a different lengths of yarn.

Challenge: Tie shells and rocks to a stick to make a wind chime.

ALUMINUM FOIL PRINTS

Theme: leaves

Skills: observing; creating

Materials: heavy-duty aluminum foil
variety of leaves

Directions:

1. Compare the different shapes of the leaves. Notice the veins and other patterns.
2. Choose one leaf, then lay a piece of aluminum foil on top of it. Pat around it gently with your hand until a print of the leaf is revealed. (You can also roll over the foil with a rolling pin.)

Challenges:

Try this project outside by making prints of tree bark, rocks, and other objects.

Make crayon rubbings of leaves, flowers, bark, and feathers. Place a piece of paper on top of the object and gently color over it with the side of a crayon. You can also do crayon rubbings on white fabric.

TISSUE FADE

Themes: colors; fading

Skills: experimenting; creating

Materials: tissue paper scraps
white paper
spray bottle or mister

Directions:

1. Tear or cut the tissue paper into small pieces (1"–2").
2. Arrange the tissue paper on the white paper. (Colors may overlap.)
3. Spray with water. What happens to the tissue paper?
4. Dry, then remove the tissue paper to see a beautiful design.

Challenges:

Cut the tissue paper into shapes or objects, such as triangles or fish.

Paint over tissue paper shapes with liquid starch and watch the colors fade.

Glue tissue paper to wax paper to make stained glass windows. (Water down the glue and use a paintbrush to apply it to the wax paper.)

COFFEE FILTER DESIGNS

Themes: colors; fading

Skills: experimenting; creating

Materials: coffee filters
water soluble markers
white paper
spray bottle

Directions:

1. Draw design on the coffee filter with the markers. (Permanent markers will *not* work.)
2. Place the coffee filter on a piece of white paper, then spray with water.
3. Dry. Remove the coffee filter to see the design.

Challenges:

Gather the coffee filter in the middle and bend around a pipe cleaner to make a butterfly or flower.

Fold the coffee filter into a cone shape, then cut out little pieces to make a snowflake.

Draw with water soluble markers on a paper towel, then spray with water.

Mix food coloring and water, then use an eye dropper to drip colors on a coffee filter or paper towel.

PAPER TOWEL DYE

Themes: color; absorption

Skills: experimenting; observing

Materials: heavy-duty white paper towels

rubber bands

food coloring

cups of water

Directions:

1. Fill the cups with one-third water. Add about ten drops of food coloring to each cup.

2. Wad up different sections of the paper towel and wrap a rubber band around them.

3. Dip the bundles in different colors.

4. Hang to dry, then open up and observe what happens.

Challenges:

Use the paper towel as a placemat for a snack, or tape together to make a wall hanging for the classroom.

Cut paper towels into strips. Color the bottom of each strip 2″ up with a water soluble marker. Dip the colored ends in a glass of water and observe which one moves up the paper towel the fastest.

Let children tie dye T-shirts with this technique. Stretch an old shirt over the mouth of a coffee can and hold in place with a rubber band. Color with *permanent* markers, then spray with rubbing alcohol. (Supervise carefully.) Watch the colors blend as the T-shirt dries.

NATURE WEAVING

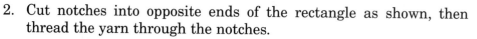

Theme: nature

Skills: observing; creating

Materials:
cardboard scraps

yarn

scissors

grass, flowers, small sticks, vines, leaves, pine needles, and so on

Directions:

1. Cut the cardboard into 8″ × 6″ rectangles.
2. Cut notches into opposite ends of the rectangle as shown, then thread the yarn through the notches.
3. Go outside and collect grass, flowers, vines, small sticks, and other items, then weave them through the yarn.
4. Attach a piece of yarn at the top to make a wall hanging.

Challenges:

What happens to the different objects as they dry?

Teach the children how to tie clovers and other wild flowers together to make necklaces, bracelets and crowns.

GARDEN ART

Themes: flowers; plants

Skills: observing; creating

Materials: flowers

heavy paper or cardboard scraps

glue

Directions:

1. Collect flowers and dry them. (Hang them upside down or spread the petals on newspaper to dry.)
2. Arrange the dried flowers on the paper, then glue them in place.

Challenges:

Add details to the picture with crayons or markers.

Use small pebbles, shells, twigs, or sand to make collages.

Dry autumn leaves and small flowers by placing them between several layers of newspaper. Pile heavy books on top, then let them dry for a week. Glue dried leaves and flowers to paper to make notecards or bookmarks.

PATTERN NECKLACE

Theme: colors

Skills: experimenting; creating

Materials:
pasta with holes
rubbing alcohol
food coloring
baggies
yarn or string
scissors
tape

Directions:

1. Divide the pasta into fourths. Put 1/4 in each baggie. Add 1 tbsp. of rubbing alcohol and a big squirt of food coloring to each bag. Shake until all the pasta is evenly colored. Dry on wax paper.

2. Cut a piece of string that will easily fit over the child's head. Tie a piece of pasta around one end so the other pieces won't slip off. Wrap tape around the other end to make it easier to thread.

3. Let children string the pasta, then tie the ends together to make necklaces.

Challenges:

Challenge children to make a pattern with the pasta.

Let children make a nature necklace by stringing flowers and leaves on an old shoelace. They can also thread shells with holes on ribbons to make necklaces, key chains, or Christmas ornaments.

© 1995 by The Center for Applied Research in Education

POTPOURRI

Themes: senses (smell); flowers

Skills: experimenting; creating

Materials:
old flowers

jars with lids

allspice, cinnamon sticks, cloves, and other spices (buy in bulk to save money)

Directions:

1. Pull the petals from the flowers and dry on newspaper in the sun for several days.
2. Layer petals and spices in the jars. Screw on the lids and allow to sit for two weeks.
3. Place in a basket or open dish for a pleasant aroma.

Challenges:

Use potpourri as gifts for parents. Place in baby food jars and let the children decorate them with ribbon and trim.

Many flower shops will donate old flowers to your classroom for art projects.

You can also purchase oils in various fragrances to use in making potpourri.

ANIMAL HIDES

Themes: animals; endangered animals

Skills: communicating; creating

Materials: brown grocery sacks
water
scissors
crayons or markers

Directions:

1. Cut the sides off the grocery bags.
2. Crumple them up. Rub them. Squeeze them. Open them up and then do it again. Keep rubbing and squeezing the bags until they are soft and wrinkled. Dip them in water, then lay them flat to dry.
3. Ask the children to draw or paint pictures of their favorite plants and animals on their pretend hides. Encourage them to discuss their pictures.

Challenges: Make a list of all the things we use that are made from animal hides.

Discuss endangered animals that people kill for their hides (alligators, tigers, seals, and so on). Should people be allowed to kill these animals? What can be done to protect the animals?

SPIDER WEB ROLL

Theme: spiders

Skills: observing; creating

Materials: dark construction paper

pie pan or cake pan

white paint

cup

spoon

marbles

salt or glitter

Directions:

1. Cut he paper to fit inside the pan.
2. Pour the paint in the cup, and drop in 2 or 3 marbles.
3. Use the spoon to put the marbles in the pan, then roll them around to make a design.
4. Remove the marbles, then sprinkle salt or glitter on the paint.

Challenges:

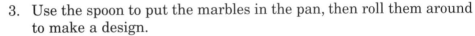

Cut paper to fit inside an oatmeal box or other canister. Add nuts, rocks, or other natural items and a spoonful of paint. Put on the top, shake, then take out the surprise picture.

Have you ever "caught" a spider web? You will need spray paint and cardboard of a contrasting color. Spray the web with paint, then gently lay the cardboard on it to "catch" the design.

FLY SWATTER ART

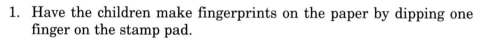

Theme: insects

Skills: observing; creating

Materials: butcher paper or large pieces of newsprint
                   stamp pad
                   fine tip markers
                   fly swatters
                   pie pans
                   paint

Directions:

1. Have the children make fingerprints on the paper by dipping one finger on the stamp pad.
2. Let them turn their prints into insects by adding detail with the markers.
3. Hang the paper outside on the fence. Pour a small amount of paint in the pan, then let the children dip the fly swatters in the paint and hit the paper with them.

Challenges:

Encourage the children to give their insects imaginary names.

Dip the eraser of a pencil in black paint and make three connected dots on a piece of paper. turn the dots into ants and other insects.

WINDMILL PINWHEELS

Theme: wind

Skills: experimenting; creating

Materials:
paper
markers or crayons
Scissors
Straight pins
pencil with an eraser

Directions:

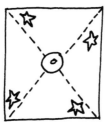

1. Cut the paper into an 8″ square.
2. Decorate both sides of the square with markers or crayons.
3. Draw diagonal lines as shown. Draw a 1″ circle where the lines cross.
4. Cut in on the diagonal lines, stopping before you reach the circle.
5. Take alternating corners and bring them into the center. Secure in place with a pin, then push the pin into the pencil eraser.
6. Hold the pencil, then blow and watch the pinwheel turn. What happens when you blow hard? Softly?

Challenges:

How are pinwheels like windmills? What kind of energy makes them both spin around? How else is wind used for energy (gliders, sailboats, and so on)?

Take the pinwheel outside on a windy day.

AIRPLANE ADVENTURES

Theme: airplanes

Skills: experimenting; observing

Materials: paper
                    paper clips
                    crayons or markers

Directions: 1. Fold the paper in half.

2. Bring front points down on each side to make a triangle.

3. Bend down the side to the bottom fold.

4. Decorate the airplane with markers and crayons.

5. Try to fly the airplane . Does it fly well?

6. Add a paper clip to the nose of the plane, then attempt to fly it.

Challenges: Experiment with different types of paper and different designs.
                    Measure how far the airplanes fly, or have contests to see who can design one that will fly the farthest.

SUN CATCHER

Themes: sun; light

Skills: observing; creating

Materials: laminating film scraps
permanent markers
hole punch, scissors
yarn

Directions:
1. Cut the laminating film into shapes
2. Decorate it with permanent markers.
3. Punch a hole at the top and add a yarn loop for a hanger.
4. Place in a window, hang from the ceiling, or hang in a tree on the playground.

Challenges: Make sun catchers from clear, plastic deli lids.

Hang several on a coat hanger to make a mobile.

BUBBLE PICTURES

Theme: bubbles

Skills: experimenting; creating

Materials: plastic bowls or margarine tubs
liquid dish detergent
food coloring
straws
paper

Directions:
1. Put a little water in the bowls.
2. Add a squirt of dish detergent to the water.
3. Have the children blow through the straws to make bubbles.
4. When the bubbles begin to overflow, add a drop of food coloring to the bubbles, then lay a sheet of paper on top.
5. What's inside the bubbles? What makes them pop? Why do they make a design on the paper?

Challenges: Try this activity outside on the playground.

Add food coloring to a bottle of commercial bubbles. Put a big sheet of paper up on the playground, then let the children blow bubbles on the paper.

PAPIER-MÂCHÉ PLANETS

Theme: solar system

Skills: communicating: creating

Materials:
books on planets
*heavy balloons
newspaper (cut in strips 12″ long)
flour and water
plastic bowl
spoon
paints and brushes

Directions:

1. Encourage the children to look at the books on planets. Note the different colors and illustrations, as well as the unique features of each planet.
2. Mix the flour and water in the bowl until it is the consistency of thick gravy.
3. Blow up the balloons and tie in a knot.
4. Cover the work area with newspapers. Take strips of newspaper, dip them in the flour and water mixture, then scrape off the excess paste and apply to the balloon.
5. Continue applying newspaper strips untill the entire balloon is covered.
6. Hang in a sunny place for several days to dry.
7. Let the children paint their papier-mâché balloons to look like different planets. Hang from the classroom ceiling.

Challenges:

What would you need to live on a different planet?

Which planet would you like to visit? How would you get there?

For Earth Week, let the children make earth balls. After making papier-mâché balloons, paint them blue, then cut out continents from green paper and glue them in place.

---

*supervise balloons carefully as children can choke on them.

CRYSTAL CLEAR

Themes: crystals; space

Skills: creating; observing

Materials: blue or black construction paper

crayons

Epsom salts

cup of warm water

paint brush

Directions:
1. Have the children draw a space picture or a picture of the sky at night with crayons.
2. Mix 1/2 cup Epsom salts with 1/2 cup of warm water and paint the solution over the picture.
3. Let the picture dry for several days, observing the crystals that form. Look at the crystals with a magnifying glass. What shape are they?

Challenges:
Paint the Epsom salts and water solution on different types of wood, paper, and so forth, and observe what happens.

Where else can you find crystals?

Pour the extra solution in a glass dish and watch what happens as it evaporates.

BODY COLLAGE—WHAT'S INSIDE?

Theme: human body

Skills: communicating; creating

Materials: butcher paper

crayons and markers

scissors, glue

yarn, straws, fabric scraps, construction paper, buttons, cotton, magazines, and other collage materials

Directions:
1. Have the children lie down on the butcher paper as you trace around their bodies.
2. Ask them to think about what they look like inside, then decorate their bodies with the crayons, markers, and collage materials. (For example, they might use the yarn as their intestines, straw for bones, cotton for brains, a picture of food for stomachs, and so forth.)

Challenges: Borrow a human model from a high school biology class for the children to examine.

Let the children go to the library and look up information of body parts.

Have the children explain their body collages and how they represented the different organs in their bodies.

INVENTION CONNECTION

Theme: inventions

Skills: experimenting; communicating

Materials: scissors, glue, tape, string, paper clips, brad fasteners, wire
boxes, plastic bottles, and other recycled materials
poster board and construction paper scraps
paint, markers, crayons

Directions:

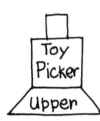

1. Ask the children what an invention is. Have them brainstorm different inventions we use every day. What would life be like without inventions?
2. Have the children think of an invention they would like to create to make their lives easier.
3. Encourage them to draw out a plan, then use the materials above to construct their inventions.
4. Let the children take turns sharing their inventions with the class and describing how they could be used.

Challenges: This project is one children might enjoy working on at home with their parents or in small groups.

Go to the library and find out more about a famous American inventor.

Write Invent America at the address below to find out how to enter children's inventions in a national competition:

> Invent America!
> 510 King Street, Suite 420
> Alexandria, VA 22314

MOTHER NATURE SCULPTURES

Theme: nature

Skills: observing; creating

Materials: wood scraps (available at construction sites or lumber yards)
natural objects (leaves, sticks, pine cones, nuts, rocks, shells, flowers)
glue
wire

Directions:
1. Go on a hike and collect natural objects for the sculptures.
2. Using the wood scraps as a base, let the children arrange the objects and glue them or wire them together to make a sculpture.
3. Encourage children to name their sculptures and describe how they made them.

Challenge: Make a class sculpture by gluing natural objects to a log or large tree stump.

SCIENCE SKETCHERS

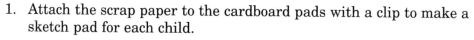

Theme: nature

Skills: observing; communicating

Materials:
scrap paper
corrugated cardboard (10″ × 12″)
clasp clips
pencils, markers, crayons or colored pencils

Directions:

1. Attach the scrap paper to the cardboard pads with a clip to make a sketch pad for each child.
2. Have the children find a comfortable place to sit on the ground. Ask them to just look and listen for a few minutes, then draw something that they like on their pads.
3. Encourage children to share their sketches with friends.

Challenges:

Relate drawings to units of study by asking children to draw trees, animal homes, the sky, and so on.

Put paper, blank books, crayons, pencils, and markers in a basket, bag, or detergent box to carry outside on the playground or on hikes and field trips.

Older children might enjoy writing poems or stories to go along with their drawings.

VII

Edible Science

Everybody loves to eat, and children will be eager to prepare the recipes in this chapter. As children cook, they are reinforcing many different science concepts, reading, implementing math skills, developing independence, and cooperating. Many of these activities can be used to introduce nutritional concepts, while others can be integrated with a particular unit of study. Feel free to reproduce these recipes on language experience charts for group experiences or turn them into rebus charts for independent activities.

As you cook with children, encourage them to use their senses, observe, make predictions, question, compare, communicate, and experiment. Have YUMMY fun!

TO MARKET, TO MARKET

Themes: food; plants

Skills: classifying; discovering

Materials: shopping list similar to the one below:

To Market, To Market!

Can you find something to eat that...

grows on a tree?
is a flower?
is a stem?
is a leaf?
is a root?
is red?
is orange?
grows in a bunch?
tastes sweet?
you eat raw?
you must cook?
starts with the letter "b"?
is big?
is little?
is round?

Directions:
1. Take the children on a field trip to the grocery store or a fruit and vegetable market.
2. Let them find fruits and vegetables that meet the above criteria. (This can also be done in small groups if you have several chaperones.)

Challenges: Make the list simpler or more difficult depending on the ability of the children in your class.

Ask children to make a list of foods imported from other countries.

Brainstorm other flowers, leaves, stems, and roots that we eat.

LUNCH BUNCH

Themes: food groups; nutrition

Skill: classifying

Materials: four lunch sacks

pictures of foods cut from 4 food groups (let children cut these out ahead of time from magazines or grocery store sale fliers.)

Directions: 1. Label the lunch sacks with the four food groups. (Add a picture clue to the word.)

2. Talk about the four food groups and let the children dictate a list of foods in each group.

3. Spread out the sacks, then let the children come up one at a time, select a food, and put it in the appropriate sack.

Challenges: Ask children to draw pictures on a paper plate of their favorite foods from each group.

Give children a lunch sack and ask them to cut out pictures of foods from each group to go in their sacks.

Find out how many servings of each group they need every day.

KITCHEN MACHINES

Theme: machines

Skills: communicating; experimenting

Materials:

egg beater

spatula

can opener

grater

potato peeler

Directions:

1. Let children play and explore with the utensils.
2. Ask children to describe how the different utensils are used in the kitchen.
3. How are the kitchen utensils like simple machines? Which one is like a wheel? A lever? A wedge?
4. What other machines are used in the kitchen to prepare food?

Challenges:

Let children beat up bubbles in a pan of water and detergent with an egg beater.

Help children prepare a snack using the different utensils.

WHAT'S FOR BREAKFAST?

Themes: food; nutrition

Skills: observing; communicating

Materials: empty breakfast cereal boxes (ask children to save these and bring them in)

Directions:
1. How can you tell how much sugar there is in the cereal you eat?
2. Pass out the cereal boxes to the children and let them look for the nutritional information.
3. Compare the amount of sugar, fat and other nutrients in the different boxes of cereal.
4. Rank the cereal from the lowest to the highest based on the sugar content. Which one would be better to eat?

Challenges:

Bring in empty cans, plastic drink bottles, and other food containers and ask the children to read the labels and compare the nutritional content.

Cut off the fronts of the cereal boxes. Punch two holes in the sides, then insert book rings to make a book that the children can "read."

FRUIT FARM

Themes: fruits; trees

Skill: classifying

Materials: basket

fresh fruits, pictures of fruits, or plastic fruits

globe

Directions:

1. Place the fruit in the basket. Ask the children to name the fruits as you remove them from the basket.

2. How does fruit get to the store? Who picked it? Who grew it?

3. Pass around each piece of fruit and talk about where it was grown. Point out on the globe the state or country where the fruit came from.

4. Discuss how different fruits grow. Which ones grow on a vine? Which ones grow on bushes? Which ones grow in trees?

5. Wash and prepare the fruits for a tasting party.

Challenges:

Find out which fruits are grown locally.

Visit an orchard or fruit farm where the children can pick their own fruit.

Take a field trip to the grocery store or farmer's market and make a list of all the fruits and where they are grown.

BEFORE AND AFTER

Themes: foods; changes

Skills: observing; predicting

Materials: grapes and raisins
peanuts and peanut butter
raw carrots and cooked carrots
apples and apple juice
strawberries and strawberry jelly

Directions:
1. Let the children taste foods fresh and after they have been processed or cooked.
2. Compare their tastes and textures "before" and "after."

Challenges: Make a list of foods you eat raw and foods that must be cooked.

Ask children to match up pictures of foods before they are cooked and after they are processed, like tomatoes and ketchup, raw eggs and fried eggs, or milk and yogurt.

GREASE DETECTOR

Themes: food; nutrition

Skills: observing; predicting

Materials:

paper towels
margarine
peanut butter
cream cheese
raw carrot
honey
pretzel
potato chip
apple slice

Directions:

1. Take two paper towels and divide them into fourths

2. Rub a small amount of the above foods in each section. Ask the children to predict which ones they think contain fat.

3. Allow the foods to set for 20–30 minutes on the towels, then examine both sides. Which foods contained the most fat?

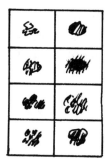

4. What happens if you eat too much fat?

Challenges:

Try this experiment with other foods that the children suggest, or let children do it with food in their lunch.

Make a list of snack foods that don't contain a lot of fat.

MILK A COW

© 1995 by The Center for Applied Research in Education

Themes: cows; milk

Skill: experimenting

Materials:
latex glove
white paint
cup of water
string
tape
broomstick
pail

Directions:

1. Prop the broomstick between two chairs. (Do this outside or cover the floor with newspaper or plastic.)

2. Mix a little white paint with the water so it looks like milk.

3. Pour the "milk" in the glove, then tie a knot in the end.

4. Tie the glove to the middle of the broomstick and poke a hole in the end of each finger with a pin. Put the pail on the floor under the glove.

5. Let the children take turns squeezing the fingers of the glove and "milking" the cow.

Challenges:

Decorate a grocery sack to look like the head of the cow and put it on one of the chairs. Make a tail from construction paper and tap it to the other end of the broom stick.

Make a poster of all the different products that come from milk.

Let the children taste different kinds of milk, such as goat's milk , skim milk, buttermilk, or chocolate milk. Which one do they like best?

TASTING WITH YOUR NOSE

Themes: senses; fruits

Skill: experimenting

Materials: grapefruit
orange
pear
apple
honeydew melon
cantaloupe

Directions:
1. Prepare bite-size pieces of the above fruits.
2. Have you ever walked in your home and could tell what you were going to have for dinner? How did you know? What sense do you use to taste food? Is there another sense that helps you taste?
3. Ask the children to close their eyes and hold their noses as you put a piece of grapefruit and a piece of orange in front of them. Let them try to identify the fruits without smelling them; then let them taste the fruits using their noses.
4. Do a similar experiment with a piece of pear and apple, or a piece of honeydew and cantaloupe.

Challenges:
How are the pairs of fruits alike? How are they different?

Why is it difficult to taste foods when you have a cold?

SWEET, SOUR, AND SALTY

Themes: senses (taste); foods

Skills: experimenting; comparing

Materials: magnifying glass
mirror
raisins
apple
lemon
grapefruit
pretzel
cracker

Directions:

1. Let the children look at their tongues in the mirror using the magnifying glass. Can they see their taste buds?

2. Cut the above foods into bite-sized pieces and give the children a small sample of each.

3. Ask the children to taste each food to determine if it is sweet, sour, or salty.

5. Encourage the children to use other words to describe the foods, such as juicy, crunchy, dry, or sticky.

Challenges: Make a "sweet and salty" snack by mixing raisins with peanuts or pretzels.

Have children sort pictures of food by their tastes.

Prepare a "white taste test" for the children. Let them taste flour, powdered sugar, salt, granulated sugar, baking soda, and cornstarch and try to identify them.

JUST BEANS!

Themes: food; graphing

Skills: experimenting; comparing

Materials: canned beans: limas, refried beans, green beans, black beans, wax beans, pinto beans, or other varieties (4–5 kinds)

Directions:
1. Heat up the different varieties of beans.
2. Let the children serve themselves a small spoonful of each. Tell them to think about which one they like most, and which one the least.
3. Draw off a grid and label it with the beans that are served.
4. Let the children color in a square by the beans they like the best.
5. Compare results.

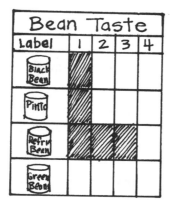

Challenges:

How are all the beans alike? How are they different?

It's fun to serve beans in a pie pan and eat them like the "cowboys."

Do tasting tests with peas, squash, and other vegetables.

Serve different kinds of apples (*Delicious, Rome, Granny Smith, McIntosh,* and so forth) and let children vote on their favorites.

PLANT EATERS AND MEAT EATERS

Themes: food; dinosaurs

Skills: communicating; classifying

Materials: celery
grapes
carrots
eggs
lunch meat (ham or turkey)

Directions:
1. Talk about how dinosaurs were divided into two groups: plant eaters and meat eaters.
2. Some animals today eat only plants, like rabbits, giraffes, and caterpillars. Other animals eat only meat, such as lions and wolves. Some animals eat plants and meat. What do plant eaters eat? What do meat eaters eat?
3. Let the children classify the above foods as "plants" or "meat," then let them decide if they want to be plant eaters, meat eaters or both, and taste the food.

Challenges: Go to the library and get a book on dinosaurs. Which dinosaurs were plant eaters? which ones were meat eaters?

Give children a piece of paper and draw a line down the middle. On one side write "plants," and on the other side write "meats." Ask them to cut out magazine pictures or draw pictures of food to go on both sides.

HUSK AND TASSEL

Themes: food: plants

Skill: observing

Materials: sweet corn (with the husk)
pan
salt and pepper
butter

Directions:

1. Show children an ear of corn in the husk and ask them if they know what it is. Where does it come from? How does it grow? (Obtain a corn stalk if possible, or show a photograph of corn growing.)

2. Point out the husk, tassel, and silk, and demonstrate how to remove them from the ear of corn.

3. Take the children out on the playground or use an old sheet and let them clean an ear of corn.

4. Boil the corn and serve it with salt, pepper, and butter.

Challenges: What are some other ways corn can be eaten?

Have the children sequence pictures of corn growing from seed, to plant, to the grocery store, to being cooked and eaten.

Children would also enjoy washing their own baking potato, wrapping foil around it, cooking it, and eating it with different toppings.

SEEDY SNACK

Themes: seeds; plants

Skill: classifying

Materials: pumpkin seeds
corn nuts
sunflower seeds
pistachio nuts
popcorn

Directions:

1. Wash your hands
*2. Place the seeds in bowls and label them. Have children serve them-selves a spoonful of each and sample them.
3. How are the seeds alike? how are they different?

Challenges:

Match up seeds with pictures of the plants they come from.

Open a coconut and taste the milk. Scrape out the meat and eat it too. Compare a coconut to other seeds.

Roast your own pumpkin seeds. After scooping out seeds from a pumpkin shell, rinse and dry them on a paper towel. Bake on a cookie sheet in the oven at 350° with a little butter and salt until toasty. You can also fry pumpkin seeds in an electric skillet with a little salt and butter.

*Very young children should not be given popcorn, nuts or other seeds, as they can choke on them.

TRASH

Theme: ecology

Skill: communicating

Materials:
flat bottom ice cream cones

fish crackers

stick pretzels

Cheerios

raisins

(peanuts and M & M's are optional)

grocery sack

Directions:

1. Wash your hands

2. Tell the story below as you dump different items into the grocery sack.

   Some people throw old fish and garbage all over, but where would you put it? That's right—in the garbage. (Dump the fish crackers in the sack.)

   Sometimes people throw sticks at each other, but where should sticks go? That's right—in the garbage. (Dump in the pretzels.)

   I know some people who just leave old tires lying all around. Where should they go? (Dump in the Cheerios.)

   Here are some old balls someone left outside. Where should they go? (Dump in the raisins.)

   (If you use peanuts, they can be cans, and M & M's can be candy wrappers.)

3. Give each child a "trash can" (ice cream cone) and put some "trash" in it for them to eat.

Challenges: Let the children make their own snack by counting out ten of each item and putting them in the ice cream cones.

Take this snack on a field trip or a nature walk, and you won't have any "trash" to throw away.

BONE BREAD

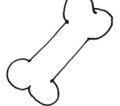

Themes: bones; dinosaurs

Skill: experimenting

Materials: frozen bread dough

vegetable oil

baking sheet

wax paper

Directions:

1. Thaw the bread at room temperature for one hour.
2. Wash your hands
3. Give each child a sheet of wax paper and place a piece of the bread dough on it for them to play with. (If the dough is sticky, let them rub a drop of vegetable oil on their hands.)
4. After the children have had time to mold the dough, let them make it into the shape of a bone.
5. Place the bones on a greased baking sheet, then bake in a 375° oven until lightly brown. (Be sure to mark the placement of each child's bone so they don't get mixed up!)
6. Serve warm. Mmmm!

Challenges:

Let children dip their bones in honey.

Talk about how the dough feels; how it smells when it's baking; how it tastes, and so on.

Tie this project in with a unit on dinosaurs by making dinosaur bones.

Mold other animals and objects from the bread dough before baking. It's fun to make letters with bread dough, too.

VEGGIE TOSSED SALAD

Themes: food; plants

Skill: experimenting

Materials:
lettuce
carrots
celery
tomatoes
cucumbers
salad dressing
ziplock baggie

Directions:

1. Wash your hands.
2. Ask the children to help clean the vegetables and cut them in bite-sized pieces.
3. Give each child a sandwich bag and let them fill it with salad ingredients of their choice.
4. Add one or two spoonfuls of dressing, zip, and toss in the air until well mixed.
5. Pour it in a bowl and enjoy.

Challenges: Offer children croutons, sprouts, and other toppings to choose from to make their salads.

Discuss what part of the plant you are eating, such as leaves (lettuce), stems (celery), and roots (carrots).

SPROUTING SANDWICHES

Theme: plants

Skills: experimenting; observing

Materials: alfalfa, radish, lentil, watercress, sunflower, or beansprout seeds
disposable dish cloth or cheesecloth
glass jar
rubber band

Directions:

1. Put 2 tablespoons of seeds in the jar, then fill it with water and allow the seeds to soak overnight.
2. The next day, cover the jar with the dish cloth or cheesecloth and rubber band it in place. Pour out the water, then cover the seeds with fresh water.
3. Place the jar on its side in a warm place where it will receive indirect light.
4. Rinse and drain the seeds twice every day for 3 to 6 days. (The seeds will need only a little water in the bottom after the first day.)
5. Expose the seeds to sunlight the last day so they will turn green.
6. Use the sprouts to make sandwiches, or put them on a salad.

Challenge: Grow several kinds of sprouts and compare them to see which ones the children like best.

SAND CASTLE CAKE

Themes: ocean; beach

Skill: experimenting

Materials:
large package of vanilla instant pudding
8 ounce container of whipped topping
milk
box of vanilla wafers
gummy sharks
clear cups
paper umbrellas

Directions:

1. Wash your hands.
2. Crush the vanilla wafers.
3. Mix the instant pudding according to the directions.
4. Alternate layers of pudding, whipped topping, and vanilla wafers (sand) in the cups.
5. Add a gummy shark and a paper umbrella.

Challenge: Make "dirt cake" in a similar way by using chocolate pudding and crushed chocolate cookies. Add sunflower seeds and gummy worms.

RAINBOW KABOB

Themes: fruits; colors

Skill: classifying

Materials: strawberries (red)

cantaloupe (orange)

pineapple chunks (yellow)

green grapes (green)

purple grapes (purple)

wooden skewers

plates, napkins

Directions:
1. Wash your hands.
2. Wash your fruit and cut into bite-sized pieces.
3. Push on one piece of fruit at a time to make a "rainbow" kabob.
4. What "color" tastes best to you?

Challenges: Roy G. Biv can help children learn the spectrum of the rainbow:

     R—*red*
     O—*orange*
     Y—*yellow*

     G—*green*

     B—*blue*
     I—*indigo*
     V—*violet*

Vary the fruits according to the season.

LADYBUG SANDWICH

Themes: insects; fruit

Skill: experimenting

Materials: red apples
peanut butter
raisins
popsicle sticks or plastic knives

Directions:
1. Wash your hands.
*2. Cut the apples in half lengthwise and core.
3. Take one half and spread peanut butter on it with a popsicle stick or plastic knife.
4. Add spots with raisins.
5. Eat your ladybug before it flies away!

Challenge: Why is the ladybug a friend to gardeners?

© 1995 by The Center for Applied Research in Education

_____

* (An adult may need to do this.)

CHEEZY CHRYSALIS

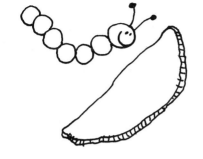

Theme: caterpillars

Skill: observing

Materials:
canned biscuits
sliced cheese
wax paper
baking sheet

Directions:

1. Discuss the life cycle of the butterfly. Read Eric Carl's book *The Very Hungry Caterpillar,* or show other books of caterpillars and butterflies. (Point out to the children that caterpillars spin a chrysalis, while moths spin a cocoon.)

2. Wash your hands.

3. Give each child a sheet of waxpaper and one canned biscuit. Have them pat out the biscuit with their hands.

4. Next, put a slice of cheese in the middle of the biscuit. Fold over the top half and press the side together.

5. Place the biscuits on the pan, noting the position of each child's chrysalis.

6. Bake according to the package directions (400°) until the cheese melts and the biscuit is light brown.

7. Cool slightly and enjoy!

Challenges:

Let the children dramatize the life cycle of the butterfly. First, let them hatch out of an egg and creep around like a caterpillar. Next have them spin a chrysalis, then let them fly out like butterflies.

Encourage the children to paint pictures of butterflies or make butterfly collages.

241

CATERPILLARS AND BUTTERFLIES

Themes: caterpillars; butterflies

Skill: experimenting

Materials: toothpicks
grapes, blueberries, or melon balls
celery
cream cheese or peanut butter
pretzel twists

Directions:

1. Wash your hands.
2. Insert blueberries, grapes, or melon balls on a toothpick to make caterpillars.
3. Spread peanut butter or cream cheese on the celery and stick in two pretzel twists for wings.
4. Wiggle the caterpillar in your mouth, then fly in the butterfly.

JUICY BAGS

Theme: fruits

Skill: experimenting

Materials: oranges
heavy-duty ziplock sandwich bags
straws

Directions:
1. Wash your hands.
2. Let the children peel their oranges and separate them into sections.
3. Place the orange sections in the baggies, seal them up, then squeeze them to make juice.
4. Insert a straw and sip!

Challenges: Try squeezing grapefruit and other fruits to make juice.
Bring in a juicer and allow the children to make different combinations of fruit juice.

FLOWERS AND STEM DIP

Theme: plants

Skill: classifying

Materials: 1 pint of sour cream or plain yogurt
1 package of dry ranch-style dressing
celery
cauliflower
broccoli

Directions:

1. Wash your hands
2. Mix the sour cream or yogurt with the dressing mix until it is well blended.
3. Have the children help wash and prepare the celery, cauliflower, and broccoli and cut into bite-sized pieces.
4. As you prepare the food, talk about what part of the plant the celery is. What part of the plant are the broccoli and cauliflower?
5. Let the children dip their "flowers" (broccoli and cauliflower) and "stem" (celery) in the dressing.

Challenge: Serve roots (carrots) and leaves (lettuce) with the dip.

244

PEANUT-PEANUT BUTTER

Theme: peanuts

Skill: experimenting

Materials:
4 cups of roasted peanuts
vegetable oil
salt
blender
crackers

Directions:
1. Wash your hands.
2. Let the children shell the peanuts and remove the skins.
3. Place the peanuts in the blender and add a little vegetable oil (1–2 tbsp.) and a little salt.
4. Blend in the blender, then spread on crackers.

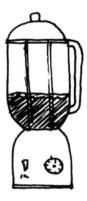

Challenges:

Where do peanuts grow? What else can you make to eat from peanuts?

Go to the library and find out all the things George Washington Carver made from peanuts.

Place 20 peanuts in a heavy-duty ziplock sandwich bag. Let children pound the peanuts between two blocks, then spread them on bread or crackers.

BANANA SPLIT

Theme: bananas

Skill: experimenting

Materials:
bananas (small)
miniature marshmallows
chocolate chips (milk chocolate)
plastic knives
aluminum foil

Directions:

1. Wash your hands.
2. Peel the banana, then slice it halfway through.
3. Stuff marshmallows and chocolate chips in the slit.
4. Wrap in aluminum foil and bake in the oven on 350° for 8–10 minutes.
5. Cool slightly. Yum!

Challenges:

You can make this same treat with the peeling on. Just put a little slit halfway through, stuff and bake in the oven for 6–8 minutes. Peel and eat.

For a cold treat, peel a banana and cut it in half. Insert a popsicle stick in one end, place it on a pan, and put it in the freezer for two hours.

MARSHMALLOW CHIPWICH

Themes: solar energy; heat

Skill: experimenting

Materials:
pie pans
aluminum foil
chocolate chips
graham crackers
hot day

Directions:

1. Wash your hands.
2. Place one graham cracker in the pie pan and sprinkle with chocolate chips and marshmallows. Cover the top with a piece of aluminum foil and seal around the edges. (Have each child write his or her name on the top with a marker.)
3. Put the pie pans in the sun and check every 10 minutes to see if the chips and marshmallows have melted. (Obviously the warmer the day, the faster this will occur.)
4. When they are gooey, place another graham cracker on top, eat, and enjoy.

Challenges:

If you don't have enough pie pans, let the children fashion their own pans from aluminum foil.

Make sun tea by placing several tea bags in a large glass jar of water in the sun for two hours.

DINOSAUR EGGS

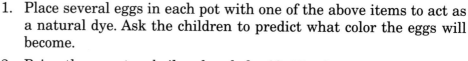

Themes: dinosaurs; eggs

Skills: experimenting; observing

Materials:
eggs
coffee grounds
beet juice
onion skins (yellow)
orange rind
5 pots spinach leaves

Directions:

1. Place several eggs in each pot with one of the above items to act as a natural dye. Ask the children to predict what color the eggs will become.
2. Bring the eggs to a boil and cook for 12–15 minutes.
3. Remove the eggs, rinse, and cool. Can the children identify the food used to make each color?
4. Let the children peel the eggs and eat them with salt or pepper if they desire.

Challenges: Were the dinosaurs born alive or did they hatch from eggs? What did dinosaur eggs look like? How big were they?

Hide the eggs on the playground for the children to find. Are they easy to find? Why? Why not?

At Easter time, dye Easter eggs with natural dyes.

ALLIGATOR PIE

Theme: alligators

Skill: experimenting

Materials: pistachio instant pudding

milk

ice cream cones (flat bottom)

plastic bowl with a lid

Directions:

1. Wash your hands.
2. Pour the pudding in the bowl, then add the milk according to the directions.
3. Seal the lid on the bowl, then pass it around for the children to shake.
4. Serve the pudding in the ice cream cones to make "alligator pie."

Challenges: Read a story, sing a song, or do a chant about alligators.

Why are alligators endangered animals? Why do some people kill alligators?

FROZEN TREATS

Theme: fruits

Skills: experimenting; comparing

Materials: bananas
grapes
fruit juice
small cups
popsicle sticks

Directions:

1. Wash your hands.
2. Give each child two cups and ask them to write their names on them.
3. Let the children slice the bananas and wash the grapes and put them in one of the cups. Have them pour juice in the other cup and insert the popsicle stick.
4. What do you think will happen if you put the cups in the freezer? (Put the cups in a jelly roll pan, then stick them in the freezer for several hours.)
5. Remove the cups and let the children taste their frozen treats. How did they change when you put them in the freezer? Are they hard or soft? Why?

Challenges: Freeze yogurt and other fruits.
Make a list of all the foods you eat that are frozen.

JELLO JIGGLE ANIMALS

Theme: animals

Skill: experimenting

Materials: instant gelatin (3 3oz. packages)

unflavored gelatin (4 envelopes)

2 cups boiling water and 2 cups cold water

shallow pan

animal cookie cutters

Directions:

1. Mix the two gelatins together.
2. Add 2 cups of boiling water and stir untill dissolved.
3. Add 2 cups cold water, then pour the jello in a shallow pan and refrigerate.
4. When the jello is firm, remove the pan from the refrigerator and let the children cut out animal shapes with the cookie cutters.

Challenges:

Use dinosaur, fish, flowers, or other shapes to correlate with a unit, theme, or holiday.

Cut an orange in half and take out the fruit so the rind remains. (Try to keep the rind in one piece.) Pour jello into the rind, chill, then slice like an orange.

OCTOPUS PARTY

Themes: ocean; octopus

Skill: experimenting

Materials:
hot dogs
plastic knives
toaster oven or hot plate
pan
(mustard or ketchup)

Directions:

1. Wash your hands.
2. Give each child a hot dog half.
3. Have them make a slice in the hot dog halfway up, then make another slice in the opposite direction. (This should make four legs on your octopus.)
4. Boil or broil the hot dogs until the legs curl up.
5. Serve with mustard or ketchup.

Challenge: How many legs does a real octopus have?

I LIKE BUTTER

Themes: milk; cows

Skills: experimenting; observing

Materials: 1 pint of whipping cream
1 plastic jar
crackers

Directions:
1. Let the whipping cream sit at room temperature for one hour.
2. Pour the cream in the jar and screw on the lid tightly. (Add 1/2 tsp. salt if you desire.)
3. Take turns shaking the jar as you pass it around the room.
4. When a soft ball of butter forms, pour off the excess liquid.
5. Chill, then serve on crackers

Challenge: Give each child a babyfood jar and pour 1/4 cup of whipping cream and a dash of salt in it. Let them shake, shake, shake to make individual servings of butter.

ANIMAL SANDWICHES

Theme: animals

Skill: experimenting

Materials: animal-shaped cookie cutters
                bread
                cream cheese
                food coloring
                raisins, pretzels, sprouts, O-shaped cereal

Directions:
1. Wash your hands.
2. Add a drop of food coloring to the cream cheese to color it.
3. Cut out the bread with the cookie cutter, then spread on the cream cheese.
4. Decorate with raisins, cereal, pretzels, sprouts, and other foods.

© 1995 by The Center for Applied Research in Education

Lion

(yellow cream cheese
raisin eyes, pretzel
whiskers, sprout mane)

Fish

(green cream
cheese, cereal eye,
red licorice mouth)

Dinosaur

(purple cream
cheese, raisin
eyes and mouth)

Challenges:

Tie these sandwiches in with a unit, story, or holiday.

Use peanut butter instead of cream cheese.

Use cookie cutter to cut out sliced cheese or meat for making sandwiches.

YIPPEE YOGURT

Theme: fruits

Skill: experimenting

Materials: vanilla yogurt
cups and spoons
fresh berries, bananas, and other fruit
granola

Directions:

1. Wash your hands.
2. Clean the fruit and cut it into small pieces.
3. Fill the cups half full with yogurt.
4. Let the children spoon berries or granola in their cups.
5. Stir and enjoy.

Challenges:

Mix plain yogurt with frozen juice concentrate. Freeze in cups with a craft stick to make a yogurt sicle.

How is yogurt made? What food group is it in?

MONKEY MISCHIEF

Theme: monkeys

Skill: experimenting

Materials: bananas
hot dog buns
peanut butter
plastic knives

Directions:

1. Wash your hands.
2. Slice the bananas and hot dog buns in half.
3. Spread peanut butter in the hot dog bun.
4. Insert the banana in the bun.

Challenges: Read the story *Curious George* by H..A. Rey. How are monkeys like human beings? How are they different?

Think of something fun you would do if you were a mischievous monkey.

© 1995 by The Center for Applied Research in Education

ZOO PICNIC

Themes: animals; zoo

Skill: classifying

Materials:
apples
celery
carrots
popcorn
berries
peanuts (in the shell)
plastic zoo animals or pictures of zoo animals

Directions:

1. Let the children share what they had to eat for breakfast. Display the animals one at a time, asking what the animals had for their breakfast.

2. Ask the children to wash their hands, then help you prepare the above foods for a snack

3. As you sample the foods, ask which animals might eat them. Can animals eat with their "hands"? How do animals eat their food?

Challenges: Put milk in bowls for children to lap up like kittens or puppies.

FRIENDSHIP SOUP

Theme: friends

Skill: communicating

Materials: large pan or crock pot

bouillon cubes

carrots

celery

corn

peas

potatoes

beans

tomatoes

onions

© 1995 by The Center for Applied Research in Education

Directions:

1. After reading the story of *Stone Soup*, ask the children if the soup was truly made from a stone. How did the neighbors help each other?

2. Tell the children they can make "friendship soup" by sharing with each other. Let them brainstorm the different vegetables they could put in their soup. Make a list and send it home to the parents, along with an explanation of what you are going to make. (You might also want to include bread and juice on the list to eat with your soup.)

3. Help the children clean and prepare their vegetables for the soup, then let them put their vegetables in the pot. Cover with water and add bouillon cubes, salt, and pepper to taste.

4. Cook the soup several hours untill the vegetables are tender. How does the soup smell as it cooks?

5. Enjoy the friendship soup with friends! (If there are leftovers, send home a small sample with each child in a baby food jar.)

Challenge: Discuss other ways friends help each other.

VIII

Weaving Science Across the Curriculum

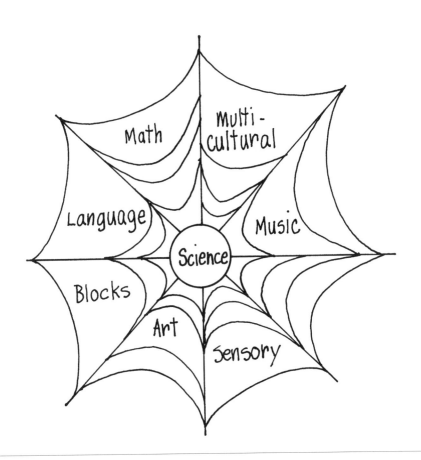

Science is really a part of everything we do with young children. From writing a story about a nature walk, to moving like animals, blowing bubbles, making music, comparing fingerprints, or having ramp races, science is an exciting way for children to learn through play. By integrating science throughout the curriculum, you can take advantage of the "teachable moment," as well as provide children with repetition and opportunities to reinforce science skills and concepts in new ways. This chapter introduces meaningful ways to incorporate science throughout your day!

GUESS WHO BIG BOOK

Theme: animals

Skills: communicating; predicting

Materials:
poster board (4–6 sheets cut in half)
2 book rings
nature magazines or pictures of animals
glue
wallpaper scraps or fabric cut in 8″ squares
markers
hole punch, scissors

Directions:

1. Cut out pictures of animals (not larger than 6″) and glue one to the middle of each page.

2. At the top of each page, write a riddle or rhyme about the animal.

3. Put glue on one edge of the wallpaper or fabric and place it over the animal to make a peek-a-boo flap. Print "who am I?" below the flap.

4. Make a title page, then punch holes in the sides of each page and put them together with the book rings.

5. Read each riddle to the children and let them predict what the animal is. Encourage them to think of all possibilities. Choose one child to lift the flap and reveal the answer.

Challenges:

Let the children make their own "guess who?" book. Have them draw a picture of an animal and dictate or write a riddle to go along with it. Tape on a peek-a boo flap.

Use paper grocery sacks to make another big animal book. Cut the front and back off the sacks to make pages for the book, and ask the children to paint or draw pictures on them. Use a verse similar to Bill Martin's *Brown Bear, Brown Bear, what do you see?* " on each page. Put the pages together with yarn or book rings.

WHO AM I?

Theme: animals

Skills: communicating; predicting

Materials: pictures of animals (mammals, fish, birds, insects)
tape

Directions:

1. Choose one child to be "it" and come to the front of the room. Have "it" turn around as you tape one of the animal pictures to his or her back. (Don't let the child see it!)
2. Turn the child so classmates can see the picture, but tell them to keep it a secret.
3. "It" goes around the room asking "yes" or "no" questions about the animal pinned to his or her back. For example, "Do I fly?" "Do I live on a farm?" "Do I have fur?"
4. When "it" has enough clues, he or she guesses the animal. If correct, another child is chosen to be the new "it." If he or she doesn't guess it, more questions must be asked.

Challenges: Make this easier for younger children by letting classmates give them clues about their animals.

Play a charades game where children act out different animals as friends guess what they are.

Take a shoe box and cut a hole in one end large enough to insert your arm. Hide different rubber or wooden animals in the box and let children stick their hands in and try to identify the animal by feeling it.

Let children take turns standing up and making different animal sounds as classmates try to guess what they are.

LOOK AND SEE

Theme: nature

Skills: observing; predicting

Materials: 9″ × 12″ clasp envelopes

pictures of plants and animals

scissors

Directions:

1. Cut several holes in each envelope as shown. (Vary the size and number of holes according to the children's abilities.)

2. Insert a picture of a plant or animal in each envelope.

3. Let the children try to identify the pictures from the parts.

4. Have them remove the pictures to verify their predictions.

Challenges:

Make a similar game using a file folder. Cut holes in the front of the folder, then tape the sides together and insert a picture.

Make a puzzle game from animal pictures. First glue the pictures to cardboard, then cut them into puzzle pieces. Pass out a puzzle piece to each child and let them find their group and put their puzzle together.

To encourage children to notice details in pictures use a "magic paint brush." Give each child a clean paint brush and ask them to paint the animals ears, nose, eyes, or other body parts.

LANGUAGE EXPERIENCE CHARTS

Themes: fields trips; nature

Skill: communicating

Materials: large chart paper
markers or crayons

Directions:

1. Take a "listening walk" with the children and tell them to use their ears to hear different sounds. When you return to the room let each child dictate a sentence to you about what they heard as you write it on the chart.

> Our Listening Walk
> Josh heard a squirrel.
> Izzy heard the wind.
> Lu heard a truck.

2. Read over the chart story together, pointing to each word.

3. Let each child read the sentence he or she contributed.

4. Have children draw pictures to illustrate the story.

Challenges:

Use languages experience charts to write up directions for experiments, art projects, or recipes.

Follow up field trips with language experience stories.

Use large chart paper when brainstorming about various topics or to write out predictions for experiments.

Have children keep a science journal of the different experiments they do and trips they take.

Directions

Predictions

263

ANIMAL STROKES

Theme: animals

Skill: writing

Materials: large paper

crayons or pencils

Directions: 1. Give each child a sheet of paper and a crayon or pencil. How does a rabbit move? Put your hand in front of your body and move your fingers in hops as the children imitate you. (Make sure to do it so it will be in a left to right direction for the child.)

2. Have the children take their crayons and "hop" them across their page.

3. Continue practicing other writing strokes by relating them to animal movements.

Animal Strokes

Rabbits hop.

Fish swim.

Elephants stomp.

Bees buzz.

Bears walk.

Challenges: Let children act out various animal movements.

Draw animal movements on sentence strips (or paper cut 3″ × 24″) and laminate. Ask children to trace over the lines with erasable markers.

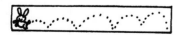

GREAT, BIG, ENORMOUS ANIMALS

Themes: mammals; dinosaurs

Skills: measuring; researching

Materials: none

Directions:

1. Take the children out on the playground and let them count as they walk off the number of feet long the following animals are:

   blue whale: 100 feet long

   African elephant: 13 feet tall

   giraffe: 18 feet tall

   tiger: 9 feet long

   brontosaurus : 90 feet long

2. Go to the library and look up dimensions on other animals.

Challenges:

Older children may want to use a ruler to get a more exact measurement.

Let the children take chalk and draw off the dimensions on a sidewalk.

Give children tape measures, rulers, meter sticks, scales, and other instruments to experiment with. Ask them to measure each other, riding toys, body parts, books, and other classroom objects.

Record children's height and weight several different times during the school year and let them compare how much they've grown.

COUNTING WALK

Theme: nature

Skill: counting

Materials: none

Directions:

1. On a nature walk or on the playground, count the number of trees, bushes, or other plants you see.
2. Count the number of animals, birds, or insects you see.

Challenges:

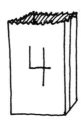

Get lunch sacks and write different numerals on them. Ask children to find sets of objects and put them in their sacks.

After collecting sets of objects, put them together, then ask children to separate them or use them to work out number stories.

Go on a letter hike where you find something for each letter of the alphabet. For example, a-ant, b-bug, c-caterpillar, d-dirt, and so forth.

© 1995 by The Center for Applied Research in Education

GUESSING GAME

Theme: nature

Skills: estimating; counting

Materials: paper and pencils

Directions:

1. Have the children estimate how many trees are on the playground. (You can use bushes, rocks, or other objects in your environment.)

2. Write down each child's prediction.

How many 🌳?

George   10

Judy   25

Ili   100

Andrew   6

3. Go outside and count the number of trees. Write the correct answer by their prediction. Was their prediction more or less than the actual number?

Challenges:

Put nuts, rocks, leaves or other natural items in a clear jar and ask the children to estimate how many there are.

Have children estimate how tall a giraffe is, then look it up in the library. How many days will it take tadpoles to turn into frogs? How many children would it take to weigh as much as an elephant?

NATURE GRAPHS

Themes: 'eaves; nature

Skills: comparing; classifying

Materials: poster board
    yardstick
    markers

Directions:

1. Prepare a grid similar to the one below.
2. Ask each child to find a leaf on the playground.
3. Compare the shapes of the leaves. Let the children place their leaves on the grid next to one with a similar shape.
4. Which one has the most? Least?

Challenges:

In the fall, graph leaves according to their color.

Graph flowers, feathers, shells, nuts, and other natural objects.

Make graphs of favorite fruits, pets, birds and so on.

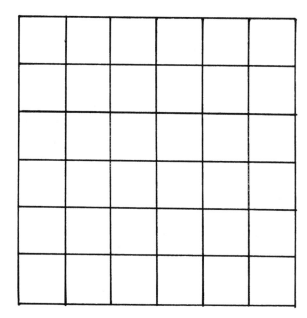

PLAYGROUND MATH

Theme: nature

Skills: sorting, patterning, comparing, seriating

Materials: natural objects (leaves, nuts, sticks, rocks)

Directions:

1. **Seriation**—Collect different sizes of rocks or sticks and have children put them in order from smallest to largest or from longest to shortest.

2. **Sorting**—After gathering leaves, nuts, rocks, or flowers, ask the children to put the ones that are alike together. Challenge children to sort the objects another way.

3. **Patterns**—Using leaves and rocks, make a simple pattern of leaf, rock, leaf, rock. Ask the children what would come next and to extend the pattern. Let children make up their own patterns with natural objects.

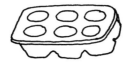

4. **One-to-one Correspondence**—Take a muffin pan or egg carton and have the children put one pebble or nut in each section.

5. **Full and Empty**—Use plastic containers, shovels, and a pile of dirt or sand to make containers full, empty, half full, and so forth.

6. **Measuring**—Let children use tape measures or rulers to measure the circumference of trees, height of flowers, length of grass, and so on.

7. **Time**—Go outside every hour and have a child stand on a designated spot. Mark the shadow with a piece of chalk and label the time. How did people use sun dials before clocks were invented?

EGG-STRA SPECIAL

Themes: human body; antibias curriculum

Skills: observing; predicting

Materials: 2 clear cups
1 brown egg
1 white egg

Directions:

1. Pass the eggs around for the children to gently hold and observe.
2. Disscuss how the eggs are alike and how they are different.
3. Ask the children to predict if they are alike or different on the inside.
4. Break each egg into a different cup and compare.
5. How are people like the eggs? Do they look alike on the outside? Are people the same on the inside?

Challenges:

Have children compare their skin and other body features. Make a language experience chart of how people are different and how they are alike.

Give children multicultural markers, paints, and crayons for art projects.

Let the children make posters and dictate stories about how they are special.

Have children use a stamp pad to make fingerprints of their index fingers. Look at them with a magnifying glass and compare them with those of classmates.

SIGN ALPHABET

Theme: senses (hearing)

Skill: communicating

Materials: copy of sign language alphabet (following page)

Directions:

1. Ask the children to cover their ears as you talk to them or give them directions. What did they hear? Was it easy to understand what was said? What would it be like if they could not hear at all?

2. How do people who are deaf or cannot hear well talk to other people? Encourage the children to talk about people they know who have hearing disabilities.

3. Introduce the sign alphabet, explaining how people who are deaf communicate with their hands. Practice making the different letters as the children imitate you.

Challenges: Learn to sing a song in sign language.

Teach the children simple sign commands you can use in the classroom, such as "yes," "no," "sit down," or "line up."

Help the children learn to spell their names using sign language.

American Manual Alphabet

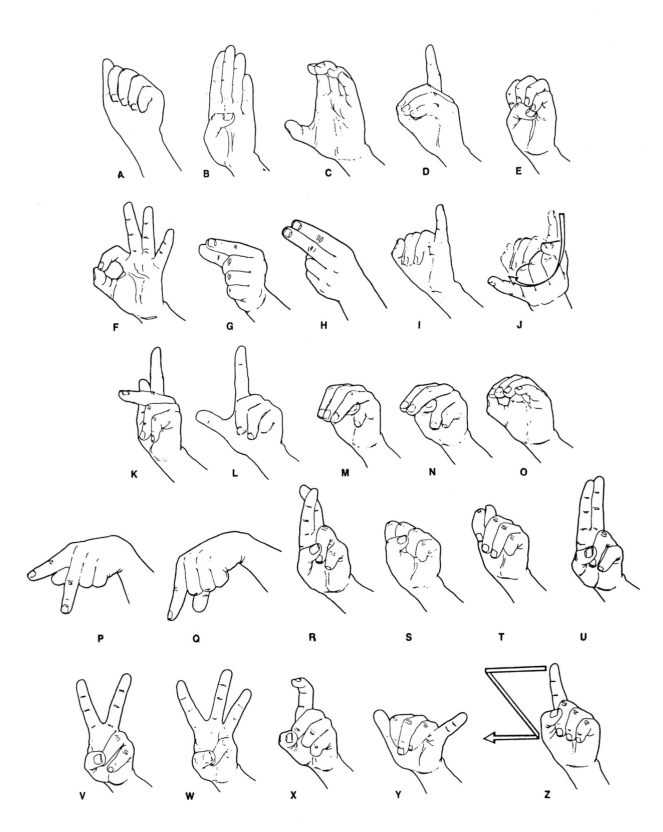

BRAILLE ALPHABET

Theme: senses (seeing)

Skill: communicating

Materials: plastic drink covers with Braille (several fast food restaurants use these)

book printed in Braille (available at the library)

poster board

glue

dried peas

Directions:

1. Have the children close their eyes and imagine what it would be like to be blind. How would they get around? How would they read?

2. Discuss how seeing eye dogs are used to help people with vision problems.

3. Pass around a book or drink cover printed in Braille. Demonstrate how people who can't see can "read" with their hands. Ask the children if they have seen Braille used in other places, such as elevators.

4. Encourage the children to talk about people they know with vision disabilities.

5. Let the children make a Braille alphabet similar to the one on the following page by gluing dried peas to the poster board.

Challenges: Ask the children to spell their names in Braille with the dried peas.

Invite someone with a seeing eye dog to visit the class.

Let the children take turns closing their eyes or wearing a mask as a friend leads them around.

Braille Alphabet

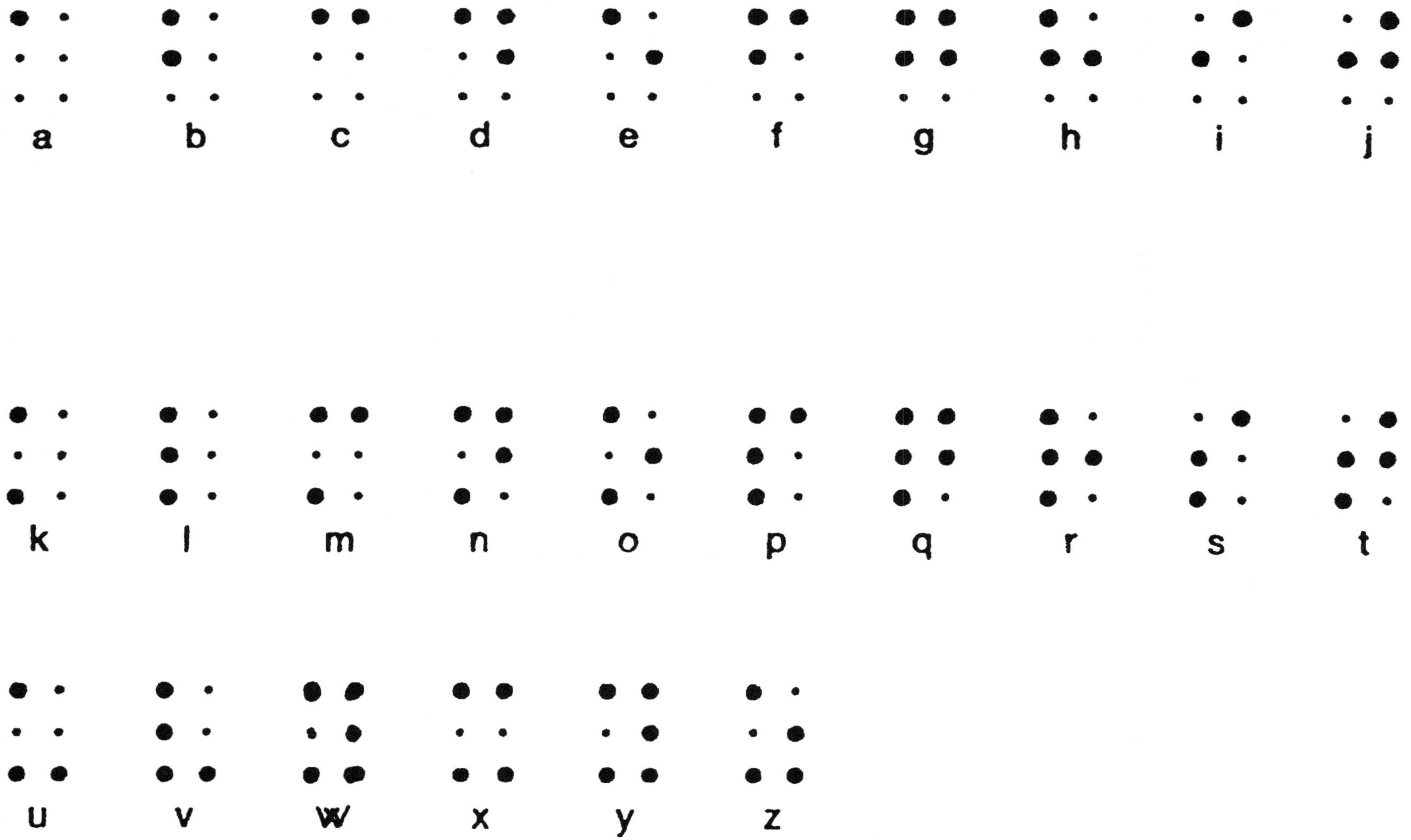

a b c d e f g h i j
k l m n o p q r s t
u v w x y z

WHEN I GROW UP

Theme: science careers

Skill: communicating

Materials: poster board

2 book rings

large sheets of paper

crayons, paints, markers

hole punch

Directions:

1. Invite parents who have careers in science to come and share with your class, or take field trips to find out what different scientists do. (Be sure to include men and women of different ethnic groups.)

2. Ask the children to think of a career in science that they would enjoy and to draw a picture of it.

3. Let the children share their pictures orally with classmates. (Older children can write a story about what they want to be.)

4. Collect the pictures and make a cover for the book from the poster board. Write "When I Grow Up" on the cover. Punch holes in the sides and insert the book rings.

5. Let the children take turns checking out the book and taking it home to share with their families.

Challenges:

Have a "dress up" day where children dress up like the scientist they would like to be when they grow up.

Discuss how teachers, homemakers, grocers, farmers, and other occupations need science skills.

Let the children put on skits or do pantomimes about their chosen careers.

Go to the library and look up information on famous nontraditional scientists.

WORLD'S BREAD BASKET

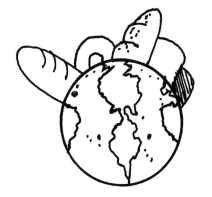

Theme: international foods

Skills: experimenting; comparing

Materials:

bagel
tortilla
croissant
matzoh
globe
French bread
cornbread
pita bread
biscuit

Directions:

1. Make a list of all the different kinds of bread they eat. Do they all eat the same kind of bread? Do people in other countries eat the same bread?

2. Show the children the above breads and point out on the globe where many people eat them.

3. Cut the bread into bite-sized pieces and allow the children to taste them. How are the breads alike? How are they different?

Challenges:

Make a graph of the children's favorite bread.

Make homemade bread, biscuits, or cornbread.

What other foods do people all over the world have in common (milk, rice, and so on).

Have an international dinner, inviting all the families to bring a dish from their native cultures.

HOMES, HOMES, HOMES

Themes:

homes; habitats

Skill:

communicating

Materials:

pictures of different homes people live in (rural, urban, suburban, mobile homes, apartments, single family dwellings, and homes of other lands)

Various blocks and building materials (straw, rocks, sticks, cloth, and so on)

Directions:

1. Show the picture of the homes to the children, encouraging them to point out the similarities and differences. How are the homes adapted to their environment? What different kinds of materials do people use to build their homes?

2. Display the pictures in the block area.

3. Encourage the children to build the homes using the blocks and other materials.

Challenges:

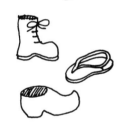

Add ethnic dolls and animals from different habitats to the block area.

Ask parents to send in different types of native dress. Compare fabrics. How does the climate influence what people wear? Why would someone need a veil to cover the face in the desert? Why would someone need a parka in Alaska?

Bring in shoes from different cultures. How are they adapted to the environment?

HARD HATS

Theme: tools

Skills: experimenting

Materials: wood scraps (available from a lumberyard or construction site)
hammer, saw, pliers, screwdriver, and so on
nails
glue
safety glasses
sandpaper
carpenter's apron
construction hats
paper and pencils
blueprints

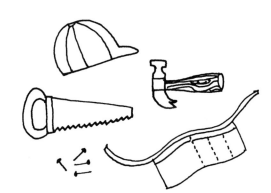

© 1995 by The Center for Applied Research in Education

Directions:

1. Introduce the tools to the children, demonstrating how to use and care for each one.
2. Encourage the children to suggest safety rules for using the tools.
3. Let the children put on the safety glasses, aprons, hard hats, and get to work!
4. Compare the tools to simple machines. For example, how are the pliers like a lever? How is the hammer like a wedge?

Challenge:

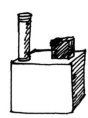

Visit a construction site and observe the tools and machines that are used.

Let children do woodworking out on the playground.

Give children cardboard boxes, tubes, styrofoam blocks, and other "junk" to construct with.

Add hard hats, aprons, and play tools to the block area.

TUBES OF FUN

Themes: tubes; tunnels

Skills: observing; predicting

Materials: clear plastic tubing (available at hardware stores)
ping-pong balls, wooden beads, golf balls, and other small toys

Directions:

1. Let the children experiment with putting the balls and beads in the tubes and observing them as they roll out.
2. Prop up the tube with blocks on the floor and roll the balls down it. Will it work if you lay the tube flat on the floor?
3. Take two different colored beads, such as red and blue. If you put the red bead in first, ask the children which one will come out first. Continue adding more beads and asking the children to predict the order in which they will come out.

Challenges: Give children cardboard tubes (from wrapping paper or laminating film) to experiment with.

Attach a clear tube to the playground fence so the children can experiment.

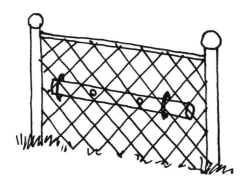

279

RAMP RACES

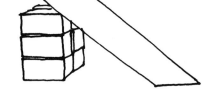

Themes: friction; incline

Skills: experimenting; predicting

Materials: 2′ × 3′ piece of plywood or heavy cardboard

blocks

sandpaper

aluminum foil

felt

waxpaper

tape

Directions:

1. Make an incline in the block center by propping the plywood or cardboard on blocks.
2. Tape sandpaper, wax paper, aluminum foil, and felt to the bottom of different blocks.
3. Which one will go down the ramp fastest? Why?
4. Let the children experiment with the blocks to test their predictions.

Challenges:

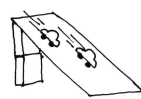

Have the children take a wet block and a dry block. Which one will be faster?

Let the children experiment with other objects in the room on ramps they construct in the block center.

Give children toy cars to race on the ramps. Which car rolls the farthest?

Brainstorm how inclines are used daily to help people do their work. What incline do they play on outside?

Demonstrate how to make a lever to catapult objects. Balance a ruler on a block. Put a paper ball on one end of the ruler and push down on the other end. What happens? Let children experiment catapulting other small, soft toys.

BLOCKS AND BONES

Themes: human body; bones

Skill: communicating

Materials: unit blocks

paper plates

crayons

Directions:

1. Ask the children to color the paper plates to look like their faces. (Make multicultural crayons, yarn, buttons, and other collage materials available to them.)

2. Have the children put their plates on the floor, then use the unit blocks to build their skeletons.

3. Encourage the children to match up the blocks to the sizes of their different bones.

Challenges:

Ask the children to find out how long they were when they were born. Cut a piece of yarn that length. Cut a piece of yarn their height now and let them compare how much they've grown.

What happens if you break a bone? Borrow an X-ray from a doctor's office for the children to observe.

39"

21"

BOATS AFLOAT

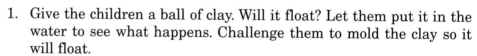

Themes: water; boats

Skills: experimenting; creating

Materials: water table, tub, or sink
clay
aluminum foil
craft sticks
toilet paper rolls
stapler
Ivory soap (bars)
metal spoon

Directions:

1. Give the children a ball of clay. Will it float? Let them put it in the water to see what happens. Challenge them to mold the clay so it will float.

2. Ask the children to make a boat from a piece of aluminum foil.

3. Let the children glue craft sticks together to make a raft.

4. Staple 2 toilet paper rolls together. Glue a sail to a craft stick and insert it between the rolls.

5. Let the children carve a boat out of the Ivory soap with a metal spoon. (Soak the shavings in water to make a liquid soap you can use to wash your hands.)

Challenges:

Give children wood scraps, styrofoam, cardboard, and other materials to use to construct boats.

Brainstorm all different types of water transportation that are used.

Float a pie pan or plastic bowl in water. How many counting bears, pennies, or rocks can you put in it before it will sink?

Show the children how to make waves in the water table with a styrofoam meat tray or piece of cardboard. Put in a boat and watch what happens to it on the waves.

FOUNTAIN PLAY

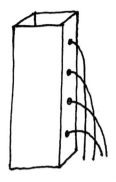

Theme: water

Skills: experimenting; observing

Materials: milk carton (quart or half gallon)
water table
nail

Directions:

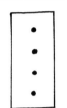

1. Poke several holes in the carton on one side from the top to the bottom as shown with the nail.

2. Hold the carton over the water table as you fill it with water.

3. Observe the amount of water that comes out of each hole. Which hole has the strongest flow? Why?

Challenges:

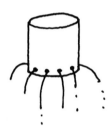

Poke holes in the bottoms of plastic bottles and other containers to make fountains to play with in the water table or sandbox.

Make a squirt station with a plastic ice cream gallon and spray nozzles from household products (window cleaner, hair spray, and so on). Hammer several nail holes in the sides of the plastic gallon. Insert the tubes from the spray bottles in the holes. Fill with water and squirt away!

SINK AND FLOAT

Theme: water

Skills: predicting; observing

Materials:

water table or tub
2 trays
variety of objects:

shells	rocks
pine cones	plastic toys
leaves	nails
sticks	metal spoon
ping-pong balls	Paper clips
cork	aluminum foil
wooden blocks	Styrofoam
wax paper	crayon
key	sponge

Directions:

1. Label the trays with the words "sink" and "float."

2. One at a time let the children choose an object and predict whether it will sink or float. After they have placed it in the water and observed it, they may put it on the appropriate tray.

3. After sorting the objects, discuss how they are alike.

Challenges:

Do this experiment outside in the summertime.

Let children do experiments with water displacement. Fill a cup half full with water. Give children some marbles and ask them to predict how many it will take to make the cup overflow. Have them do water displacement experiments with different containers and different objects, such as rocks and ice cubes. What happens to the level of the water when you get in the bathtub? Why?

Wad up a paper towel and put it in the bottom of a clear cup or glass. Turn the cup upside down and insert it in the water. What happens to the paper towel? Why doesn't it get wet?

WATER WAYS

Theme: water

Skills: experimenting; observing

Materials: water table or tub
food coloring
glitter
liquid detergent
flavorings and extracts (vanilla, mint, perfume)
ice cubes
fishnet
plastic bottles
funnels and measuring cups
baster and eye dropper
toy dishes
baby dolls, doll clothes
paint brushes

Directions:

1. Fill the tub or water table with water, then add food coloring, glitter, fragrance, liquid detergent, or ice cubes to the water for different sensory experiences.

2. Give the children the fishnet and let them scoop up plastic toys with it.

3. Let the children wash doll clothes, baby dolls, or toy dishes.

4. Give the children the funnels, measuring cups, baster, and other objects to experiment with.

Challenges:

Freeze large chunks of ice in plastic bowls. Put the "icebergs" in the water table along with plastic arctic animals (seals, walrus, polar bears, and so on.)

Freeze colored water in different containers and add it to the water table.

Tie the ends of a piece of yarn that is 30″ long into a knot to make a necklace. Put one end in an ice cube tray, freeze, then remove to see your "frozen jewel."

DIRT PLAY

Themes: soil; plants

Skill: experimenting

Materials:
water table or small tubs
potting soil
shovels
plastic flower pots
artificial flowers
plastic fishing worms

Directions:

1. Put the potting soil in the water table or tubs.
2. Let the children play in the dirt with the shovels, flower pots, artificial flowers, worms, and other props.

Challenges:

Add water to the soil and let the children make mud pies.

Hide clean bones in the dirt and have the children be "paleontologists" and dig them out.

Spray paint rocks and pebbles gold, then let children "pan" for them in the dirt.

Mark off a special area on the playground where the children can dig in the dirt. When the children are tired of playing with the potting soil, use it to plant seeds.

RAINBOW RICE

Theme: color

Skill: experimenting

Materials: rice
rubbing alcohol
food coloring
plastic bags

Directions:

1. Ask each child to bring in a small bag of rice
2. Have the children put their rice in a plastic bag. Add 1 tbsp. rubbing alcohol and a big squirt of food coloring to the bag and then let the children "shake it up." Spread on wax paper to dry.
3. Mix all the colors together in the water table or other tub to create rainbow rice.

Challenges:

Give children measuring cups, spoons, and other containers to fill and measure. Ask questions such as, "How many spoonfuls of rice does it take to fill the cup?"

Store rice in plastic bags or covered containers to use over again. Rainbow rice can be put in plastic bottles to make musical instruments, or it can be used for mosaics in art.

BIRDSEED TO BEANS

Theme: sensory materials

Skill: experimenting

Materials:
water table or tubs
bird seed
dry beans
pasta (cooked or raw)
oatmeal or cornmeal
confetti or cotton balls
shaving cream
measuring cups and spoons
plastic containers
cardboard rollers
funnels
play dishes

Directions:
1. Put one of the above sensory materials in a water table or tub.
2. Add props and toys.

Challenges:

Let the children play with the birdseed outside in the winter. The birds will enjoy everything that spills on the ground!

Combine sensory materials, such as beans and rice.

Fill the water table with such "seasonal stuff" as autumn leaves, flowers, snow, shells and sand, pine straw, and so on.

Place rice, beans, cornmeal, and other sensory materials on old lunchroom trays for individual play. Add plastic animals, cars, toy people. and other props.

SILLY PUTTY AND GLOOP GALORE

Theme: sensory

Skills: experimenting; communicating

Materials: included in all recipes

Directions: Have children help you make one of the recipes below. Encourage them to describe how it feels as they create.

Silly Putty

1 cup glue (not school glue)

1/2 cup liquid starch

Slowly stir the starch into the glue. Knead it with your hands (Add more glue or starch until it is the right consistency.) Store in a covered container in the refrigerator.

Add food coloring

Make individual portions by mixing 2 tbsp. glue with 1 tbsp. liquid starch in a small cup. Store in a plastic egg.

Gloop

1 package unflavored gelatin

3/4 cup water

Put the water in a pan and sprinkle the gelatin on top. Stir over medium heat until the gelatin dissolves and the mixture comes to a boil. Cool and chill.

Add food coloring.

Make a larger batch by adding 4 packages of gelatin to three cups of water.

Mud Dough

2 cups mud

3 cups sand

1/2 cup salt

Mix the ingredients with enough water to make pliable. Form objects or use cookie cutters to cut out shapes.

SILLY PUTTY AND GLOOP GALORE
(*continued*)

Homemade Bricks

dirt or clay

straw or grass

milk cartons

petroleum jelly

Mix the dirt with straw and water until it is thick goop. Grease the sides of the milk carton with petroleum jelly, then add the dirt mixture. (Fill the carton 1" or 2" deep.) Bake in the hot sun for several days, then peel off the carton.

Squeeze Bags

ziplock sandwich bags (heavy duty)

shaving cream

cornstarch and water mixture

gloop (from previous page)

hair gel

media mixer

mud

duct tape

Fill the baggies with one of the above materials. (Reinforce the seal with duct tape.) Let the children squish and squeeze the bags.

Squirt shaving cream in a bag, then add a drop of red and yellow food coloring. Seal it up and let the children "make orange." (Add other primary colors to make secondary colors.)

BUBBLICIOUS FUN

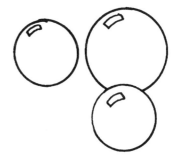

Themes: bubbles; air

Skills: experimenting; observing

Materials:
Dawn dishwashing liquid
pipe cleaners
berry baskets
toilet paper rolls
plastic rings from drink cans
fly swatter
straws
string
large bowl

Directions:

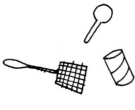

1. Mix 1 cup *Dawn* detergent with approximately 4 cups water. (You may need to experiment with the amount. It should be strong enough so when you make a circle with your fingers it will form a bubble you can blow.)

2. Bend the pipe cleaners into bubble wands.

3. Use the toilet paper rolls, fly swatter, berry baskets, and other objects to experiment blowing bubbles.

4. Cut a straw in half. Take an 18″ piece of string, thread it through the straws, and tie the ends together. Holding the straws, immerse the strings in the bubble solution. Gently pull through the air to form giant bubbles.

Challenges:

What is inside the bubbles? Why do they pop?

Make individual bubble solutions by mixing 1/2 cup water, 1 tbsp. detergent, 1 tsp. glycerin, and 1/2 tsp. sugar in a small cup.

Another solution for giant bubbles can be made by mixing 2 cups *Joy* with 6 cups water and 3/4 cup white *Karo* syrup.

MAKING MUSIC

Themes: senses (hearing); music

Skills: experimenting; communicating

Materials:
toilet paper roll	plastic bottles
wax paper	rice, popcorn kernels, beans, and macaroni
rubber bands	paper plates
shoebox, paper towel roll	stapler
oatmeal canister	

Directions:

1. Make a kazoo by decorating a toilet paper roll with markers or crayons. Cut a 9″ circle from wax paper and rubber band it to one end of the kazoo. Punch a hole with a pencil 1″ from the other end, and then hum a tune into the kazoo.

2. Stretch rubber bands over an empty shoebox to make a guitar. Attach the paper towel roll for a handle.

3. Make a drum by beating on an oatmeal cannister or similar container with the end of a pencil or your hand.

4. Shakers can be made by filling plastic bottles with rice, popcorn kernels, beans, macaroni, or other objects.

5. Color two paper plates and staple them together 3/4 of the way around. Fill with 1/2 cup of macaroni or beans and staple closed. Shake like a tambourine.

Challenges:

Ask children to look around their homes for other objects that can be used like instruments.

Fill glass bottles or drinking glasses with varying amounts of water. Strike with a metal spoon to make different sounds.

© 1995 by The Center for Applied Research in Education

ALLIGATOR

Theme: endangered animals

Skill: communicating

Materials: none

Directions: Have the children repeat each line of this chant about endangered animals after you.

Alligator

Chorus: *Alligator,*   *(Say with a quiet voice.)*
Alligator,   *(Say with a medium voice.)*
Alligator,   *(Say with a loud voice.)*
Can be your friend, can be your friend,
Can be your friend, too. (Say fast.)

The alligator is my friend,
And he can be your friend, too.
If only you could understand
Don't wear him as a shoe!

(Chorus.)

The manatee is my friend.
He likes to swim and float.
If only you could understand,
Don't hurt him with your boat.

(Chorus)

The elephant is my friend.
He works from dawn to dusk.
If only you could understand,
Don't take his ivory tusk.

(Chorus.)

The bald eagle is my friend.
He likes to fly around.
If only you could understand,
Don't destroy his nesting ground.

(Chorus.)

Challenge: Make up other verses for different endangered animals.

293

ANIMAL RACES

Animal Races

Theme: animals

Skill: motor development

Materials: pictures of animals (bears, ducks, birds, horses, rabbits, monkeys, fish, crabs, and elephants)

Directions:
1. Have the children line up behind a designated line. Show them an animal picture and ask how that animal moves. Choose one child to demonstrate.
2. Let the children move like that animal to a goal and back. Suggested movements are:

   bird: flap arms like wings

   duck: grab ankles and waddle

   horse: gallop

   fish: make swimming stroke with arms

   rabbit: jump on two feet

   bear: put hands down on the ground and walk on all fours

   monkey: scratch sides with arms

   elephant: bend over and make a trunk with arms

   crab: lean back on arms and move backwards on all fours

Grrr!

Challenges: Do relay races using animal movements.

How do animals talk to each other? Make animal noises as you move around. How would you sound if you were an angry lion? A happy bear? A frightened bird? A proud horse?

Play unique musical selections and have children move like those animals. (You might use *The Flight of the Bumble Bee, The Elephant Walk, Galloping Horses,* or *The Octopus's Garden.*)

Tell children to think of an animal that walks, one that flies, and one that swims. When you call out "land," "sea," or "air," they must move like that animal to a designated line and back.

IX

Growing Together

Parents are indeed their child's first and most important teacher. This chapter capitalizes on that principle, as well as the importance of the home/school relationship, with activities that can be copied and sent home to parents. These "parent pages" can be attached to weekly newsletters, or bound together to make a book to use over vacation times. Be sure to ask parents and children for feedback; then use their responses to help you create additional activities they can do using other ideas in this book.

Dear Parents,

There are so many exciting ways you can help your child learn at home.
In the weeks to come, you will be receiving an activity page similar to this one
with experiments, art ideas, and recipes that will open the door to science discoveries for you and your child. Children are 'natural" scientists who are full of
questions, curiosity, and a sense of wonder about the world in which they live.

So have fun learning and growing together!

Sincerely,

SCIENCE KIT

You will need:

a detergent box with a handle

magnifying glass

flashlight

ziplock bags

a shoebox , or cloth bag

small mirror

magnet

paper and pencil

Directions:

1. Fill the box with the above tools.
2. Show your child how to use the magnifying glass, magnet, flashlight, and other tools.
3. Help your child collect leaves, flowers, and other objects from nature in the bags.
4. Encourage your child to draw pictures of what he or she sees.

Just for fun!

Let your child decorate the outside of the box with crayons, markers, paint, or scrap paper.

Take the science kit on a nature walk. Turn over a log and look at insects with the magnifying glass. Can you find anything that the magnet will attract? Draw a picture of the clouds in the sky.

Talk about a scientist you know and what that person does.

SENSE WALKS

You will need: lunch sack

pretty day

Directions:

1. Go for a walk outside with your child. First, use your eyes and talk about all the things you see. Look up, down, and all around.

2. Stop and close your eyes. What sounds do you hear? Can you hear any animals?

3. Use your nose. Can you find something that smells good?

4. Find something that feels soft. Find something that feels rough. Hide something in the sack, then see if your child can identify it by feeling it.

5. Fix a snack when you get home and use your sense of taste to enjoy it.

Just for fun!

Take a tape recorder and record different sounds that you hear.

Draw a picture of all the things you see when you get back home.

Take a walk at night. Do you hear different sounds? Does it feel different at night? Why do things look different at night?

WORLD WATCHERS

You will need:

2 cardboard rollers (from toilet paper)

tape or stapler

hole punch

yarn or string 26″ long

crayons or markers

Directions:

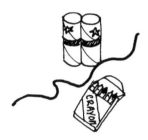

1. Tape or staple the two rolls together.
2. Punch a hole in the top of each roll on the side, then tie the string in the holes. (Make sure the string is long enough to easily slide on and off your child's head.)
3. Let your child decorate the binoculars with markers or crayons.
4. Have your child look out the window at all the wonderful things in the world, or take the binoculars on a walk.

Just for fun:

Count how many different animals your child can find with the binoculars.

How many different plants can he or she find?

Look for pictures in the clouds.

HIKER'S PACK

You will need:

large paper grocery sack

velcro or tape

scissors

stapler

2 strips of fabric or ribbon cut $1'' \times 24''$

crayons or markers

Directions:

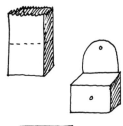

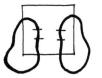

1. Cut off three sides of the grocery sack halfway down as shown.

2. Take each strip of fabric or ribbon and tie the ends together to form loops. Staple the loops to the back of the bag to create shoulder straps.

3. Fold over the top of the sack to form a flap on the backpack. Add a piece of velcro or tape so it can open and close.

4. Let your child personalize his /her backpack with name and pictures.

5. Put a snack or lunch in the hiker's pack, or, use it to collect leaves, rocks, and other "treasures" you find on a nature walk.

Just for fun:

Think of other things you can make from grocery sacks, such as masks, vests, and books.

NATURE BOOK

You will need:
5 ziplock sandwich bags

2 twist ties (from bread wrappers)

feathers, leaves, flowers, seeds, shells, or other natural objects

Directions:

1. Go outside and hunt for natural objects, such as feathers, leaves, seeds, or flowers.
2. Put one object in each baggie and zip it closed
3. Poke two holes in the side of each bag with a pencil.
4. Put the bags together with twist ties to make a book.

Just for fun:

Write the name of each object on a piece of paper and put it in the baggie.

Let your child tell you a story about the different items. Encourage the child to tell you where it comes from, how it feels, what color it is, and so forth.

NATURE BOX

You will need: plastic salad or deli container

magnifying glass

Directions:

1. Give your child the container when you are going on a nature walk or when he or she is outside playing.

2. Let your child put glass, sticks, rocks, flowers and other natural items in the container.

3. Sort the objects that are alike with your child.

4. Let your child look at the objects with a magnifying glass.

5. Encourage your child to return the objects to where they were when he or she is through looking at them.

Just for fun: Think of an art project children can do with the objects in the box. For example, they might want to glue the leaves and flowers to a sheet of paper.

Use the box to hunt for specific objects in nature, such as leaves , nuts, or rocks.

LEAF RUBBINGS

You will need: paper

old crayons

leaves of different shapes

Directions:

1. Collects different kinds of leaves

2. Take the paper off an old crayon

3. Lay the paper over one leaf and gently rub the side of the old crayon over it to make the outside of the leaf appear. (It works best if you color in one direction.)

4. Make rubbings of other leaves.

Just for fun:

Help your child learn the names of the trees and what trees the different leaves come from.

Make rubbings of the bark on trees, or use flowers, pine needles, rocks, and other objects to make rubbings.

Try making a rubbing on a piece of white fabric, then use it for a napkin or place mat. (If you put a piece of wax paper over the crayon print and iron it with a hot iron, it will help seal in the color.)

BIRD FEEDER

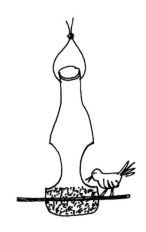

You will need:

clear plastic bottle from vegetable oil (you can also use a milk jug)

scissors

birdseed

string

Stick 12″ long

Directions:

1. Cut two "windows" out of the side of the bottle.
2. Punch two holes near the bottom of the bottle just below the windows. Insert the stick in the holes to act as a perch for the birds.
3. Poke two holes near the top, then tie on a piece of string to make a hanger.
4. Fill the bottom with birdseed or breadcrumbs.
5. Hang the bird feeder from a tree or near a window.
6. Be a bird watcher!

Just for fun:

Go to the library and check out a book that will help you identify the birds in your yard.

Put out different kinds of food and observe to see which one the birds like best.

Here's another easy bird feeder you can make. Mix peanut butter with a little sand. (This will help the bird digest the peanut butter and keep from choking.) Spread the peanut butter mixture on pine cones or large pretzels and sprinkle with birdseed. Hang with a piece of string from a tree.

POPCORN PLANT

You will need:

clear jar or glass

popcorn kernels (popcorn you buy at the grocery store to pop will work)

paper towel

sand or soil

Directions:

1. Fold the towel in half, then place it in the jar next to the glass.

2. Fill the inside of the jar with sand or soil.

3. Push several popcorn kernels down between the paper towel and the side of the jar.

4. Water the kernels, then set the jar in a sunny window. (Give your child the responsibility of watering the plant every three to four days or when it gets dry.)

5. How many days before you see a root? How long does it take before you see a stem?

Just for fun:

When the popcorn grows larger, plant it outside in your garden.

Look around your kitchen for other seeds you can plant. You might try dry lima beans, apple seeds, an avocado, or the seeds from other fruits.

SHINY PENNIES EXPERIMENT

You will need:

pennies (old ones work best)

vinegar

salt

cup

spoon

Directions:

1. Put 1/2 cup of vinegar in the cup.
2. Stir in 1 tbsp. of salt.
3. Let your child drop the pennies in the cup, then stir them around, counting to 25.
4. Take the pennies out of the cup and rinse them off in water.
5. Taa-daa! Shiny pennies just like magic!

Just for fun:

Soak the pennies in lemon juice and observe what happens.

Will the salt and vinegar solution work on old nickels and dimes? Try it and see.

DANCING RAISINS EXPERIMENT

You will need:

small raisins

clear soda or ginger ale

glass

Directions:

1. Fill the glass with soda.
2. Ket your child drop 4 or 5 raisins in the glass.
3. Watch the raisins. What happens to them? Look very closely to see if you can discover why they dance up and down.

Just for fun:

Will raisins bob up and down in water or apple juice? Try it and see what happens.

TIN PAN BAND

You will need:

pie pan

wooden spoon

2 plastic bottles with lids

macaroni and rice

cardboard roller

Directions:

1. Hit the pie pan with the wooden spoon to make a drum.
2. Fill one bottle with 1/2 cup of macaroni, and fill the other bottle with 1/2 cup of rice to make shakers.
3. Hum into the cardboard roller to make a horn.
4. Put on some music and let your child march around or dance, playing the different instruments.

Just for fun:

Look around the house for other things you can use for instruments.

Take your child to a concert, or listen to some classical music on the radio.

CUP PHONES

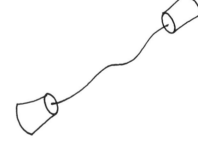

You will need:

2 paper cups

2 paper clips

5′ piece of string

Directions:

1. Poke a hole in the bottom of each cup with a pencil.
2. Thread one end of the string through the hole in the bottom of each cup.
3. Tie a paper clip to each end of the string in the cups.
4. Let your child hold one cup to his or her ear as you talk in the other cup. (Pull the string taut as you talk.)
5. Take turns talking and listening. How does the sound travel from one cup to the other?

Just for fun:

Place your hand on the speakers of your radio or television and feel the vibrations from the sound.

WAVE BOTTLE

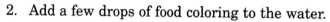

You will need: 1 plastic bottle
vegetable oil
food coloring
water

Directions:

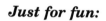

1. Fill the bottle with 2/3 water.
2. Add a few drops of food coloring to the water.
3. Fill the bottle to the top with oil, then screw on the top tightly.
4. Let your child turn the jar on its side and gently roll it around to make waves.

Just for fun: Shake the jar up. Why does the oil always float to the top?
Add small shells or glitter to the bottle.

CHANGES! CHANGES!

You will need: photographs of your child from infancy to the present (4 or 5 photos will work)

Directions:

1. Show children their baby pictures. Did they have teeth or hair? Could they play or talk?

2. Ask your children how they've changed since they were babies. How have their bodies changed? What can they do now that they couldn't do when they were younger?

3. Let your children sequence the pictures showing how they've grown from babyhood to the present.

4. Talk about what they will be like when they grow up. What do they think they will look like? What will they do when they're adults that they can't do now?

Just for fun:

Record your children's height on a growth chart or closet door. Make sure you mark the date.) Show them how tall they were when they were born. Continue recording their height every six months.

Talk about how other things grow and change, such as trees, flowers, and animals.

BUBBLES OF FUN

You will need: liquid detergent (*Dawn* works best)

water

pail or pan

berry basket, fly swatter, plastic ring from drink pack

Directions:

1. Put 3 cups of water and 1 cup of detergent in a pail or pan.
2. Stir. (Add enough detergent so a bubble will form when you make a circle with your fingers.)
3. Go outside an let your child experiment making bubbles using the berry basket, fly swatter, and plastic ring.

Just for fun:

Cut off the toe from old hose and stretch it over one end of a cardboard roll. Dip the end with the hose in the bubble solution, then blow in the other end and watch the bubbles flow.

Use pipe cleaners, coat hangers, straws, and other objects to make bubbles.

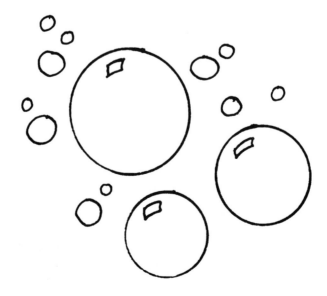

WORLD'S BEST PLAY DOUGH

You will need:

1 cup flour

1/2 cup salt

1 cup water

1 tbsp. vegetable oil

1 tbsp. cream of tartar

food coloring (several drops to desired color)

Directions:

1. Mix the above ingredients together in a pan.
2. Stir until smooth.
3. Place on the stove and cook over medium heat, stirring constantly.
4. When the dough forms and sticks to the spoon, remove it from the heat.
5. Knead.
6. Let your child mold the play dough into different objects.
7. Store the dough in a plastic bag or air-tight container.

Just for fun:

Give your child cookie cutters, a plastic knife, safety scissors, and other tools to play with.

Experiment by making different colors of play dough. Add red and yellow to make orange, or add blue and red to make purple.

Give the play dough a scent by adding a few drops of food flavoring, such as vanilla or almond.

JUNKY CREATIONS

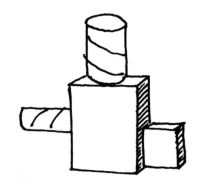

You will need: empty cardboard boxes
cardboard rollers
recycled aluminum foil
plastic tubs and cartons
other "junk" you usually throw away
masking tape

Directions:

1. Save the food boxes and other containers from your house for one week.

2. Give your child the "junk" and challenge him/her to make a sculpture or invention from it.

3. Ask him/her to think of a name for the "junky" creation.

Just for fun: Start a "recycling" center" around your home by saving paper, plastic, aluminum, glass, and other materials you often throw away.

Take your child to a recycling center.

Look for the 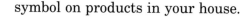 symbol on products in your house.

SPACE PUDDING

You will need:

ziplock sandwich bag

instant pudding

milk

measuring cup

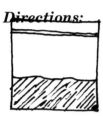

Directions:

1. Wash your hands.
2. Put 2 tbsp. of pudding mix and 1/3 cup of milk in the bag. Zip it up.
3. Have your child squeeze and squish the bag for several minutes until the pudding thickens.
4. Poke a small hole in the corner of the bag, then let your child suck it out like an astronaut.

Just for fun:

Talk about how astronauts eat food and why they have to eat it that way.

To make a frozen "space pop," put a marshmallow on a wooden stick. Fill a cup with pudding, then insert the stick with the marshmallow. Freeze for seven hours, peel off the cup, and you'll have a space pop.

EENSY WEENSY SPIDER SANDWICH

You will need:

2 slices of bread

peanut butter

pretzel sticks

raisins

plastic cup or circle cookie cutter

Directions:

1. Wash your hands.
2. Show your child how to cut circles out of the bread with the cup or cookie cutter.
3. Let your child spread peanut butter on one slice of bread.
4. Put the second slice of bread on top and add raisins for eyes and a mouth.
5. Give your child 8 pretzel sticks to add for legs.
6. Mmmm! Eat it up!

Just for fun:

Sing *The Eensy Weensy Spider.*

Talk about why spiders weave webs. Can you find a spider web outside?

How many legs do spiders have?

BUGS ON A LOG

You will need:

celery

cream cheese

raisins

Directions:

1. Wash your hands.
2. Clean the celery and cut it into 3″ pieces to make "logs."
3. Let your child spread cream cheese in the hollow of the celery "log."
4. Give your child several raisin "bugs" to put on top of the cream cheese.

Just for fun!

Spread peanut butter or pimento cheese on celery for a healthy snack.

Look for bugs in your yard and observe them to see what they do.

Resources
from A–Z

Field Trips

Guest Speakers

Materials and Equipment

Inexpensive or Free Materials

Science Resource Books

Where can you order science materials and equipment? What are some science field trips you can take? Whom can you invite to be guest speakers? What are some organizations you can contact for additional information and free literature? Are there other science books for teachers you might be interested in? Answers to these questions and more can be found in this chapter.

SCIENCE FIELD TRIPS

aquarium

botanical garden

college science department

dairy

farm

farmer's market

fish hatchery

Forest preserve

hardware store

high school science department

hospital

laboratory

library

lake, river, or ocean

natural history museum

orchard

pet shop

planetarium

plant nursery

recycling center

science museum

school playground

state park

veterinarian's office

water treatment plant

weather station

zoo

GUEST SPEAKERS

astronomer

biologist

chemist

conservationist

Cooperative Extension Service Agent

dentist

doctor

engineer

farmer

forest ranger

gemologist

geologist

health professional

meteorologist

nutritionist

veterinarian

SOURCES FOR MATERIALS AND EQUIPMENT

Bio Quip
17803 LaSalle Avenue
Gardena, CA 90248

Carolina Biological Supply Company
2700 York Road
Burlington, NC 27215

Edmund Scientific Company
101 East Gloucester Pike
Barrington, NJ 08007-1380

Insect Lore Products
P.O. Box 1535, 132 South Beech Street
Shafter, CA 93263

NASCO
901 Janesville Rd., P.O. Box 901
Fort Atkinson, WI 53538-0901

Nature Watch
P.O. Box 1668
Resada, CA 91337

MAGAZINES FOR CHILDREN

Falcon Magazine
(Conservation Magazine for Children)
P.O. Box 1718
Helena, MT 59624-9948

OWL
Owl Communications
179 John Street, Suite 500
Toronto, Ontario
Canada M5T3G5

Ranger Rick
(Children 6–12)
National Wildlife Federation
1400 Sixteenth St. NW
Washington, DC 20036-2266

Your Big Backyard
(Preschoolers 3–5)
National Wildlife Federation
1400 Sixteenth St., NW
Washington, DC 20036-2266

ORGANIZATIONS

(Sources of Inexpensive or Free materials)

Endangered Species Commission
1849 C Street NW
Department of the Interior, Room 4429
Washington, DC 20240

Environmental Protection Agency
401 M Street SW
Washington, DC 20546

NASA (National Aeronautics and Space Administration)
300 E Street SW
Washington, DC 20546

National Arbor Day Foundation
100 Arbor Avenue
Nebraska City, NE 68410

National Audubon Society
940 Third Avenue
New York, NY 10022

National Geographic Society
17th and M Streets NW
Washington, DC 20036

National Park Foundation
1101 17th Street NW, Suite 1102
Washington, DC 20036-4704

National Science Foundation
4201 Wilson Blvd.
Arlington, VA 22230

National Science Teachers Association
1840 Wilson Blvd.
Arlington, VA 22201-3000

National Wildlife Federation
1400 16th St. NW
Washington, DC 20036

U.S. Fish and Wildlife Service
c/o Department of the Interior
1849 C St. NW
Washington, DC 20240

U.S. Forest Service
c/o Department of Agriculture
Fourth St. and Independence Ave. SW
Washington, DC 20250

RESOURCES FOR TEACHERS

Brown. S. *Bubbles, Rainbows, and Worms*. Mt. Rainier, MD: Gryphon House, 1981.

Carlson, L. *Eco Art!* Charlotte, VT: Williamson Publishing, 1993.

Claycomb, P. *Love the Earth*. Mt Rainier, MD: Gryphon House, 1991.

Cobb, V. *Science Experiments You Can Eat*. New York, NY: J.B. Lippincott, 1972.

Cohen, R., and Tunick, B. *Snail Trails and Tadpole Tails*. Mt Rainier, MD: Gryphon House, 1993.

Cornell, J. *Sharing Nature with Children*. Nevada City, CA: Dawn Publications, 1979.

Feldman, J. *Survival Guide for Preschool Teachers*. West Nyack, NY: Center for Applied Research in Education, 1990.

Forte, I. *Science Fun Nature Crafts*. Nashville, TN: Incentive Publications, 1985.

Kohl, M., and Gainer, C. *Good Earth Art*. Bellingham, WA: Bright Ring Publishing, 1991.

Mitterman, Passineau, J., Schimpt, A., and Trent, P. *Teaching Kids to Love the Earth*. Duluth, MN: Pfeifer-Hamilton, 1985.

Moore, J., and Evans, J. *Simple Science Experiments*. Montery, CA: Evan-Moor. 1987.

Pieffer, W. *The World of Nature*. Bridgeport, CT: First Teacher Press, 1990.

Recyclers Handbook. Berkeley, CA: Earth Works Press, 1990.

Rockwell, R., Sherwood, E., and Williams, A. *Hug a Tree*. Mt. Rainier, MD: Gryphon House, 1986.

Sherwood,E., Williams, R., and Rockwell, R. *More Mudpies to Magnets*. Mt. Rainier, MD: Gryphon House, 1990.

Thurman-Veith, J. *Natural Wonders*. Palo Alto, CA: Monday Morning Books, 1986.

Williams, R., Rockwell, R., and Sherwood, E. *Mudpies to Magnets*. Mt. Rainier, MD: Gryphon House, 1987.

INDEX